M000222563

Real Estate Investing

Master Commercial, Residential and Industrial Properties by Understanding Market Signs, Rental Property Analysis and Negotiation Strategies

Copyright 2018 by Michael K Brown - All rights reserved.

This document is geared toward providing exact and reliable information in regards to the topic and issue covered. The publication is sold with the understanding that the publisher is not required to render an accounting for official permits, or for other qualified services. If advice is necessary, legal, or professional, a practiced individual in the profession should be contacted.

- From a Declaration of Principles which was accepted and approved equally by a Committee of the American Bar Association and a Committee of Publishers and Associations.

In no way is it legal to reproduce, duplicate, or transmit any part of this document by either electronic means or in printed format. Recording of this publication is strictly prohibited, and any storage of this document is not permitted unless written permission is granted by the publisher. All rights reserved.

The information provided herein is stated to be truthful and consistent, in that any liability, in terms of inattention or otherwise, by any usage or abuse of any policies, processes, or directions contained within is the solitary and utter responsibility of the recipient reader. Under no circumstances will any legal responsibility or blame be held against the publisher for any reparation, damages, or monetary loss due to the information herein, either directly or indirectly.

Respective authors own all copyrights not held by the publisher.

The information herein is offered for informational purposes solely and is universal as such. The presentation of the information is without a contract or any type of assurance guarantee.

The trademarks that are used are without any consent, and the publication of the trademark is without permission or backing by the trademark owner. All trademarks and brands within this book are for clarifying purposes only and are owned by the owners themselves and are not affiliated with this document.

Published by Pluto King Publishing

ISBN 978-1-989711-06-4 (Paperback)

Table of Contents

Disclaimer

Although investing in real estate can be an intriguing option for earning money, you must be aware of the risks involved with holding a real estate investment. All properties on the market may be subject to losses.

Talk with a financial advisor or other consultant before getting into this field of investing. Discuss your plans for investing and review all risks carefully. Be advised that there are no guarantees that your investment plans will result in a profit. All real estate properties are at risk of losing their value.

Be aware of the assets you have on hand before you get into an investment as well. The expenses associated with investing in real estate may be very high depending on what you plan on utilizing for your investment desires.

The information in this book is intended for general information purposes only. This book does not provide any legal or tax advice. The author and publisher disclaim any liability in connection with the use of this information.

Ask a tax professional or other financial expert for additional assistance if necessary or to see what might apply within your specific situation.

The writers, producers and sellers of this guide cannot be held responsible for any problems that might come about during the investment process. Be cautious with how you invest in a property and for how you take care of its physical features. Be aware of what you may do with any tenants who get into a space as well.

Also, the points listed in this guide are made with investors in the United States in mind. Most of the content is universal and can be utilized in Canada, the United Kingdom or other countries that people can invest in. However, the rules might vary by country. Check with the laws in the country you wish to invest in to learn more about how you can invest in a property.

Introduction

Investing is a thrilling activity that gives people the opportunity to make large amounts of money. This is all about purchasing assets in the hopes of making money off of them. People have been investing in various assets for generations with varying levels of success. However, it is a big part of life that no one can truly resist. Investing is all about finding ways to take one's money and stretch it out as well as possible.

Because the investing field is so massive, it is often a challenge to try and find something that you might want to invest in. You could invest in practically anything from new business endeavors to commodities that are traded and used on the daily market. The options are vast, but in the end, it is up to you to figure out what you should put your money in. One option you can consider when finding an investment entails real estate.

The exciting world of real estate investing is something anyone could enjoy entering into. When you invest in real estate, you are working with a property that can be high in value and could easily become profitable depending on how you run it. You could restore the property or even rent it out to other people. You will often have full control over what you want to do with your property.

The best part of investing in real estate is that you can get any kind of property that you want on the market to work for you. You could not only find a traditional home but also a larger commercial or industrial space that you might be interested in. Whatever it is you have a desire for, you can surely get it on today's market.

In order to get the most out of real estate, you have to know what you are doing when investing in it. You have to identify what properties are best for investment purposes and what you can get out of them. You must also understand what is available for your use on the market.

This guide includes information on everything relating to how to manage real estate. This includes a look at different types of properties you can utilize, how you can get a property ready and so forth. The information includes many details relating to how you can find a great property and what to figure out when finding something of value.

You will also learn about not only how to plan your offers for a property but also what to see before you actually place your offer out on the market. Some properties might have hidden issues that need to be resolved. Others might simply need to be inspected to see how much they are worth. You can even work with foreclosed properties or even acquire property through the auction block.

Additional points on negotiations and taxes are covered in the guide as well. You will also learn about what you can do to quickly increase the value of any property you invest in. Points of being a good landlord for any tenants you wish to incorporate into our property investment are covered as well. The extensive information featured within this guide will help you to identify everything you need to know about the market and what you can get out of it.

The overall process involved in this guide might take weeks or even months for you to carry out. Your real estate investment is something you cannot afford to short-change. You have to work as hard as possible to show others that you are serious about a deal and that you really want to get into the real estate market. Knowing what to do to make any deals you do work out right in your favor helps as well.

All the points included in this guide will help you see what you can get out of a quality property. Be sure to see what is listed here so you have an easier time with finding a property you will want to stick with. Besides, there is always a great chance that you might get a good profit off of the market. But it will only work when you understand what you are doing while having a strong plan in place for getting a property that you want.

Chapter 1: Getting Into the Investment Scene

Everyone has their favorite things in which he or she likes to invest. Some people invest in stocks and bonds. Others like to stick with commodities. One thing is for certain -anything could be worth investing in. All a person needs to do is find something where the value is surely going to change.

The goal of any investment is to buy low and sell high. It is a simple routine that makes investing all the more inviting and worth trying. Best of all, there is no real way to tell how high something could rise in value. Then again, there is also the chance that the investment might decline in value.

The buy low-sell high mantra is a point that can be said about real estate in particular. You might have read stories over the years about real estate properties changing in value. You could have even heard about how the real estate market is a barometer for the entire economy. That is, the economy might be in good standing when real estate values increase. Sometimes a property might even be worth twice its value down the line.

The world of real estate investing has been growing over the years. People are learning more about how to find real estate. They are starting to recognize the tax benefits of investing and how the market works. The online world has made it easier for people to invest too, as people are able to find properties through various websites. Even reality television programs about investing in individual properties have helped get the industry to grow and thrive.

Investing in properties can be worthwhile provided a property is managed correctly and you understand the signs in the market. The potential for you to make a sizable profit in the real estate market could be great, although you would have to look at many market factors.

This guide is all about helping you make the most out of your real estate investment plans. You will learn about many aspects relating to finding properties and how to get more out of a transaction. You might be wondering why real estate investing is such a good idea.

Why Get into Real Estate Investing?

You have many options to choose from when you decide to invest. Getting into the real estate market is not something to take lightly. It costs lots of money to enter that investment field. When finding a property you wish to invest in, you will have to carefully look at the many options in the market. You will have to put in more effort into finding real estate than any other type of investment. So what would make you want to enter this particular investment market?

The reasons for getting into real estate investing are plentiful. You will benefit from investing if you learn all you can about the field and study how to make money in real estate.

Protect Yourself from Inflation

Inflation is a vital concern that must be considered when you a look at anything you wish to invest in. This refers to the rate at which the cost of living is increasing. The purchasing value of money will start to decrease when prices of different goods start to increase. To some, it is an annoyance when the prices of different products on the market suddenly going up in value and cost more to buy. However, it is actually a very important concern worth exploring.

Inflation is a natural part of any economy. The problem is inflation rates could outpace the returns on your other investments. This could be a real problem depending on what you are making from those investments. For instance, you might be earning interest in your bank account if you have lots of money in that account. Have you ever considered that the interest rate in that account might be less than the inflation rate? The power of whatever you have in your account might be minimal after a while.

Real estate is a worthwhile investment because it protects you from the serious effects of inflation. As the economy expands and inflation increases, the values of properties will also increase. Rents go up and the prices for other properties in an area increase as well. The potential for real estate to move alongside a traditional inflation rate is strong as there will be no need to worry about your investment decreasing in value over time due to this natural part of the economy.

High Tangible Asset Value

The tangible value of a property refers to the physical value. The value specifically relates to things that someone can actually touch and experience. A real estate property has a high tangible asset value because it is something that people can use. In other words, you have a complete physical hold over the asset you are investing in.

The tangible values of assets on the investment market are often not as great as you might wish. For instance, a commodity investment like oil or livestock might not have tangible value. This comes as you don't actually have literal possession of barrels of oil or possession of livestock. You only have contracts that allow you to sell a certain amount of a commodity at a particular rate at some point in the future. With a real estate investment, you have full control over some special property of interest to you. You will be able to physically control that asset in any way you see fit.

Real estate properties always have values attached to them. This is different from many other assets that don't have any tangible values. There is a potential that an asset that does not have a tangible value might decline in worth as the demand for it becomes too low. For instance, a traditional stock does not have much of a tangible value because there is always the potential the value might go down to zero. This could happen if the demand is low enough so that stockholders would sell off their stocks. You would not have much control over what the company in which you own stock can do either. It could be easy for the company's stock to decline dramatically without much warning.

Property and the land it is based on will always have some kind of value attached to it. There is no real chance that the value of it would disappear. There is always some use and value for a property. People will have a need for a property regardless of its value and what it is worth at any time. The potential for such a property to be valuable and for it to stay active and viable is always strong. As you will see throughout this book, there are many things that will directly impact the tangible value of a property.

It should also be noted that a real estate property, unlike some other tangible assets, has a better chance of its tangible value increasing. Real estate is designed to last for generations. An investment will not decrease in value over time. A vehicle will eventually wear out and break down in time. Real estate will last forever if managed correctly and taken care of properly.

Tax Benefits Are Available

You can also take advantage of various tax benefits when you invest in real estate. This is something that will be covered later in this guide, but it is a point worth checking. You could get various tax deductions on some of the many things associated with your property investment. These deductions

33

can be very valuable and will keep you from losing large amounts of money on your investment due to those taxes. There are various rules and stipulations associated with the tax benefits, so learn what you can do and when you can do it.

Works For a While

Another big part of why so many people invest in real estate is because they can use real estate as something to hold onto for years. Nowadays, we hear lots of stories about people trading stocks and bonds rather quickly. People often try to unload stocks as soon as possible if they hear of any problems or concerns with their investments. Just think about the many stories about people who have lost large amounts of money on their investments because they did not act quickly enough to sell them before they declined in value.

Real estate investing is different. You will not have to worry about massive short-term declines or sudden issues that might cause the value of a property to drop dramatically. Real estate is a long-term investment. You could hold the property for years and not have to sell off your investment at all if that's what you want.

Either way, you will not likely experience issues where the value of your property suddenly drops like what might happen with traditional stocks and other investment choices. It takes a while for a transaction to be completed, thus keeping people from trying to trade properties too quickly. There is no real way property values could decline quickly because people are trading properties in all areas at the same time.

A Focus on Control

One huge reason real estate investing is special is because the investor has full control over what is done with the property and how well the property can make money. You can choose to restore it, expand it, let other people use it, and so forth.

Many of the things you can do with your property could help increase its value.

This is much more interesting than just sticking with stocks. The problem with stocks is that you don't have any say in what the business associated with the stock can do. There is always a chance that the business might collapse or have legal trouble. It might experience reduced sales totals. Even worse, some businesses that offer stocks might not be forthcoming in what they are doing, thus making it harder for you to find out if you're making the right call.

With real estate, you have say over what you can do with the property. You can choose to do anything as long as it abides by your contract and any district rules relating to that property. You would have to check on the terms of your property and the contract to see how you can increase its value. No matter what you do with the property, you will find that it is not hard to get this investment to work for you with few or no problems. You can easily invest in real estate and not struggle with problems relating to how much control you have over your investment.

The History of Investing In the Market

While many people are talking about real estate investing these days, this is a practice that has been going on for years. In fact, the real estate investment industry has been active for longer than you might think. Specifically, it is impossible to figure out precisely when the market started initially.

What we do know is that the concept of landlords has been around since antiquity. It is believed that early people would provide funds in exchange for shelter in certain places.

The establishment of the free market system in western society helped to make real estate investing popular. Although it is difficult to discover how the field evolved, it is known that investments were used by early people as a means of new wealth. Those who owned more properties were often considered to have more power and control over their society.

People would often value properties based on how large they were, how prestigious those areas might be, and what those areas could be used for. Details on precisely how valuation standards were put into place are unclear, but the basic principles used today have been utilized in some form for generations.

The early part of the 20th Century saw real estate investing becoming really important, not only to the rich but to the middle classes as well. The growth of the United States population and the expanding influence of capitalism on the American economy helped make the real estate industry popular. The rise of suburban housing in the mid-20th Century helped make investing in property popular. This came as the market grew as more people were looking to buy homes to raise their families. Some of the suburban communities around cities helped create definitions or standards about how properties and neighborhoods were to be organized.

The Federal Real Estate Investment Trust act of 1960 helped make the investment field all the more attractive. With this, large investors began gathering their resources together to support extensive real estate projects. This made it easier for them to acquire properties or to offer them to the public. The act has been revised a few times since it was introduced, but it has been critical for ensuring that the real estate investment market would continue to grow and thrive.

The rise of home improvement television programs in the late 20th Century made investing in homes all the more popular. This gave rise to people looking to acquire and restore old homes to sell them for a profit. The public television program 'This Old House' set off a new interest in home improvement projects to make properties better and more attractive. This also led to a sea of television programs devoted to many aspects of taking care of homes. Even reality television has joined the mix as many shows are being made which highlight people doing what they can to make their properties more attractive and useful.

The history of real estate investing is still evolving as more people are looking than ever before to find attractive properties. Developing your own investment plan could be interesting and worthwhile financially. Once you start investing in real estate, you will realize why so many people love doing it. Investing is more than just a hobby. It is something that could bring you riches if you understand what you are doing and you make the right decisions.

An Option to Diversify One's Portfolio

Real estate investing can help you create a diversified portfolio. You might have heard in the past how important it is for you to have a diverse and varied portfolio. Having a good variety of investments is vital so you can reduce the risk in your investments. Investments are different based on their values and how they perform on the market. Commodities are clearly different from stocks, for instance.

Real estate helps you to create a diverse portfolio as it entails a new market to work with. The real estate industry is different based on how money changes and shifts. When you invest in real estate, you will work with a different type of investment that operates separately from the stock market. Be aware of how the value of the real estate you invest in changes, as it could decline in value even when the market goes up. Then again, there is also a chance that the value will increase even when the overall economy is struggling.

A Versatile Field

Real estate investing is popular because it has a versatile and diverse array of properties for you to buy. You can stick with traditional homes or even larger properties that require multiple tenants. You could own a property where you choose to either improve its condition or rent it to tenants. Sometimes you just might focus more on your own property that you wish to live in yourself. Whatever you have in mind for investing, you will find that it is easy to get into the real estate investing field and to potentially make a good deal of money in the process.

You can also invest in commercial and industrial properties. These include properties where retailers or businesses will rent your property from you. Some of these properties could work for retail or office operations – the possibilities are endless.

What can happen in the real estate investment field is worth exploring. Investing in properties will keep your portfolio diverse and unique. The potential profits that come from the field of real estate investing are worth investigating. The important thing is to plan carefully and make the right investments.

Chapter 2: What Is Real E li Investing?

The concept of real estate investing has been around for generations. Some people think that it is just about buying and selling property. That is technically an important aspect of the field, but unlike other investments, you have some sense of control over what you hold. The variables that can directly impact the real estate market can be significant.

There are many aspects of real estate investing that need to be explored. You must understand everything that goes into real estate before you try to take advantage of the field.

The General Concept

Real estate investing is a practice where a person will acquire a home or another property. That person could hold onto the property for an extended period of time. In some cases, that investor has full rights to the property regarding what can be done with it. In other cases, the investor might have full control over the buildings and the land that the property entails, thus adding to the assets that one has for use.

The general goal of real estate investing is to sell the property in the future at a profit. An investor will need to find a way to sell the property after its value increases. This could come from either the natural increase of the property's value or from any improvements that have made to the property. Sometimes the value can increase when enough tenants use the property. This includes not only having enough renters but also having them remain as renters for a long while.

This is an exciting field that you can participate in with many types of properties. You could get this to work with a traditional home or from a commercial building that is used an office building or shopping center. Whatever it is you find, you might get something exciting out of your investments.

An International Affair

Checking your local market is essential as there are many options to choose from no matter where you are. You could invest in real estate in any part of the world. Every part of the world has some kind of real estate that you could invest in. You just have to search to see what can be of use to you can.

Do you want a vacation home in Sri Lanka and rent it out to people who need a place to stay while in the area? Do you want to invest in a strip mall in Atlanta or some other city with a growing economy? It does not matter where the property is located. You have the option to invest in anything so long as you check out what is available. You can always stay with your local market if you prefer, but having the option to find real estate in another corner of the world is always something worth thinking about.

You have to be aware of the rules associated with investing in a property in another country. These include rules about what can be done with a property and the tax laws for that country, and even if you can own property as a foreign buyer. Details on choosing between a local or long-distance property will be covered later in this guide.

A Long-Term Focus

Real estate investing focuses on long-term needs. While many different investments are ones that could change quickly, real estate is something that increases in value over time. You might hold onto a property for several years before you actually sell it. It might take a while for you to sell a property, but it could be worthwhile when you actually get to that point.

To understand this, you have to look at how a real estate transaction is different from a traditional stock purchase. Real estate requires research and analysis plus an extensive contract and maintenance to keep a property in the best shape possible or to find the right tenants. It could take years for the property investment to be worthwhile when everything is considered.

A regular stock purchase is very different. In this case, you would simply have to research a business and then execute a trade within a few minutes. You could then sell that stock in a few hours if you wish if you see that the price is rising. This simplicity of trading makes it possible to quickly acquire or trade it rather fast. This is not always the best thing in the world because the trading volume on something can be high. An investment like this might change in value quickly. It is also easy for people to develop strong emotions when trading stocks; they might let their emotions cloud their common sense.

With real estate, you will not have to worry about the value of your investment changing dramatically. The market has less liquidity, meaning that people cannot enter and leave it quickly. It takes a while for some properties to change in value. This is a good thing as it gives you time to plan your strategy for investing and for deciding on ways to make your property more valuable and attractive to others.

The intricate and specific nature of the real estate market is also one that requires far more research and investigation than other fields. You have to spend a long time investigating which properties are right for your investment. It can take some time to find the right property, but the rewards will be great when you find one that you want to invest in.

Restore or Improve Properties

The things you can do with your real estate property are varied. You can choose to restore a property that might have seen better days. One of the main reasons why people invest in real estate is because they know that they can make their properties increase in value when restorations are done. A property might get into disrepair over time and therefore be rather cheap to buy because many people may not see the value or may not want to actually live in it.

When a property is restored, it may become inhabitable for a while. What the restoration process often entails is massive renovations to make it useful and habitable. In such a case, the value of the property will increase. This could produce a sizable profit depending on how extensive and expensive the renovations are.

Even more importantly, renovations will make the property safer. The value of a property will increase when it is stable and safe to live in. The risk of further damages or even the outright collapse of the structure will be eliminated or at least significantly reduced. This, in turn, gives you a better chance to make a profit from the property.

People can also buy properties to make improvements and make them more valuable. An extension could make a property larger and more useful. Sometimes an existing room might be redone and used for a new intention. A new detached building could be added to a property in some cases. This could add a great space for more improvements provided the property includes the surrounding land or lot and if the owner has the legal right to add a new building.

Introducing New Properties

Some real estate investments might entail more than just structures. You could also invest in the land around a property. You might be able to acquire an empty plot of land and have the option to build something new on the land provided it follows the zoning standards and any other rules for construction in that local area.

You could build a new building on your land or plot and then use it to increase the value of your investment. The new building could be used for your new dwelling, for someone else to live in, or you could rent the property out. There's also the option to set up a business site or even a farm or ranch depending on what the zoning laws for that area are. The possibilities you have for a great property are limited only by the rules to which your plot of land would be subjected.

This is a thrilling endeavor, but it would require a lot of research to help you see what you can do with the property. You would also have to determine the amount of money you would have to spend on building something on the land. The chances for you to make big money are good, but you would have to plan everything diligently for it to be a profitable enterprise.

Manage Many Tenants

A good thing to realize about real estate investing is that it often involves working with tenants. You do not have to live in the property you are investing in. Rather, you can manage a property that will house a tenant or two or even more. Best of all, this part of investing is versatile as it could work with many kinds of properties. These include both commercial and residential properties.

Tenants come in many forms:

1. An entire house - people can rent it for a certain period of time.

2. A larger apartment building - appropriate for many tenants to pay rent.

3. An office building - for multiple corporate entities to provide you with rent.

4. A single-occupant commercial property - one business running its operations out of a large building and lot. That occupant could pay more rent if it had full access to the entire building and/or more land to work with.

5. Industrial properties - might include many people renting out certain areas for their separate businesses.

Having a tenant for your property is a great way to make money. You have to make sure to do background checks to screen renters properly. Additional information on how to be the best landlord will be covered later in this guide.

You have the option to work with one of many types of properties when earning money from your investment. You do not necessarily have to get a tenant but it could help you when your aim is to make money.

How Can You Make Money?

Let's talk about the reason why you are reading this guide – you want to enter the real estate investment field because you want to make money. It is clear that you could make a sizable profit from investing in real estate properties. You could make tens of thousands of dollars from a property depending on how you choose to invest and in what you invest. The following are some ways to make money from your real estate investment.

Increase in Value

Your real estate could increase in value over time depending how much other properties in an area are worth, how well a home has been restored or improved, and so forth. Sometimes the general market in your area might be a factor with inflation often causing the value of some properties to increase. Sometimes the surroundings in a local area might be a big factor. You will learn more throughout this guide about the many ways the value of a property can change.

Restoration or Flipping

The restoration or flipping process is something to investigate to make money from a property. Flipping is buying a property, restore or repair it, and then sell it for an increased selling price. You would have increased the value of the property as its condition is better than what it had been before.

It is an exciting endeavor, but it could also be hard to manage. You would have to spend money to repair the structure. It could take months or even years for the process to be fully completed. The timing varies based on how many repairs have to be completed and how intensive the restoration process might be like. However, when the property itself is fixed properly, it becomes easier for the property to increase in value.

Income from Rent

You can also have a rental income you collect. Rental income can be derived from people who want to live in your house, one of your apartment units, or from a commercial building that houses retail or office space. The rent can be collected on a monthly basis or any other schedule you wish to establish.

Income from Commissions

You might also earn income from commissions you earn from people buying into your property. You might get people to buy properties you have to sell and you will be able to also charge commissions on the sale. A commission is a fee associated with getting your property sold if you sell it yourself.

You will earn more when you convince someone to buy into your building or a portion of the property. You could sell one part and receive a commission from it based on what you are charging for the transaction.. This could add to the possible profits you make.

Additional Items on Your Property

You might also derive additional income from anything added to your real estate property. These include items that you might charge extra for people to use. An example of this is how apartment complexes use laundry facilities. A complex might offer a washer and dryer for everyone's convenience. These could be coin-operated models. This could be paired with a vending machine that dispenses detergent and other items needed for doing laundry.

It could also make money by having vending machines in the building. These include machines for various items for personal use or even snacks and soft drinks. The chances for a profit could be great provided the machines are regularly stocked.

The key for such features in a real estate property is to find ones that people might actually use. The laundry example is great because everyone in the building will have to use the facilities at some point in the week.

You could also charge people for using certain spaces within the building. Perhaps an apartment building has a private basketball court. That court might be open to the public. You could incorporate the use of that court into the rental fees. You could even charge people for when they want to reserve an area for a special private event. This allows you to make money from something on your property while still giving people the option to use that space.

Real estate investing is a thrilling and viable option to look into when finding a way to make money. The potential for you to get a great profit from any real estate you wish to invest in could be significant. As you will see in the next chapter, the options you have to work with are extensive.

Chapter 3: Types of Real Estate You Can Invest In

Now that you know how you can make money by investing in real estate, you can think about the types of investments you want to do. You have the option to invest in practically any kind of structure or land area. Nothing has to be too large or small. How do you decide which type of property or land is right for you to invest in?

The world of investing is popular because a person can invest in practically anything. Every major investment category has its own variety of things you can work with. When you invest in stocks, you have the option to invest in any kind of stock from any publicly listed company. Real estate investing is the same because you could invest in one of many types of properties.

Not all real estate properties are equal. You would have research some of the options available to decide on something you wish to invest in. Each property is different.

Residential Properties

The first type of real estate property you could invest in is property for residential use. Residential properties are those properties used for living purposes. People can choose to either live in the properties they buy or to rent them out on a month-to-month basis.

Some people need larger properties for all the members of their families. Others buy property for their retirement needs. There are even cases where people might find properties for vacation use or recreational purposes. There are smaller residential properties that are suitable for a single person.

You can invest in one of many properties that are designed with specific housing needs in mind. No two residential properties are ever alike. These properties have many forms:

- Basic homes are the most common types of homes. These are properties not attached to anything else. The single-family home is the most prominent type of home.

- Apartments, flats, and condos are properties that have many units that people either rent out to others if they own the entire building or which can be sold individually. People who live in these types of buildings may have to pay condo fees as well.

- Terraced homes are full-sized homes but are attached to each other. One building could be several homes together. In most cases, you might have control of just one home in a terraced property. In other instances, you could acquire the entire building and rent out individual homes to renters.

- Larger ranch areas might be appealing. Usually these properties are away from other traditional homes and they require their own special zoning rules for them to be built, lived in, or rented.

Every residential property is different based on size, usage, location, and other factors. You will read more about how residential properties can be used later in this guide.

Commercial Properties

Some of the more popular properties for investment are commercial properties. These are large properties that have many uses. They could work for office areas or for retail purposes. A commercial property has to be used for business purposes.

Individual Retail Properties

Some of the more popular real estate properties include single-tenant buildings. These include places where one business is responsible for operating the building. This could entail just one store inside a larger complex or a standalone property. Whatever the case might be, you can find many retailers and businesses to occupy such a property.

Some commercial properties have space for just one business. A supermarket might be a good example of this. A larger anchor department store could also be housed in its own separate building. There are no strict rules for how large or small a commercial retail store has to be; it could be large enough that there is only one client in the single retail property.

Larger Retail Complexes

Some of the other retail properties include large retail complexes that feature many tenants. This could be like a traditional apartment complex but with businesses. That is, the businesses would pay you rent for using your property. They may also work with their own design standards for keeping their businesses unique although some rules can also be set for how individual stores have to look similar to one another in the same complex.

A retail complex could include a small strip mall that features multiple properties in one area. You could also buy a larger shopping mall that can handle dozens of business. Commercial properties are versatile as they can be designed in many ways and can house as many or as few tenants as needed.

The options you have for investing here are vast. The type of anchor you would work with might make a huge impact on how well the investment works for you. An anchor could not only provide you with a larger amount of money but also the potential to bring in other commercial tenants that might want to share the same area. Regardless of what the case might be, it helps to investigate the possibilities of how well an anchor might work in a larger commercial area.

Office Properties

An office property could be a valuable option for commercial buildings. An office property is different as it is not a place that works with retail goods. It is rather a place that offers some kind of service to the community.

An office property can be designed so that many people can work there. You can set up a property with a floor plan that features offices for high-end management positions and other areas for workers to work and congregate. The property can be laid out in any way that the office requires. The key is to figure out how many people should the property accommodate and what configuration would make working there easy. This could be designed in cooperation with the office management.

You also have the option to decide the number of tenants you want to have situated in that building. You can choose to have just one business to work with a single floor plan. In other cases, you can have multiple sections divided with each section being devoted to a different business. You could even allow businesses to share the same floor plan and work in the same physical building.

Commercial properties are enticing because they normally involve longer leases. It might also be easier for you to get businesses to buy into those properties because these places are usually easy to fill. There will always be a need for businesses to find accommodations set up operations. In fact, not all tenants in an office building have to be local. Larger national or international businesses could set up satellite offices in some of these buildings too.

However, you have to be careful how a property is filled and what businesses you choose to invite as renters. It is important to look at where an office building is located and if it has enough features for individual tenants to be interested. They might want to find buildings that offer online connectivity features and enough room for not only private meetings but also for open work environments. Every business has specific demands for what it requires of an office.

The returns from such office properties might vary based on the operating costs and the number of tenants it can comfortable accommodate. Remember, the quality of the building and its location are important factors whether or not people will want to rent the building and use it.

In addition, the general economy might be a factor in deciding what the property is worth. A growing economy is one where people are more likely to reserve office space with you. Businesses will want to set up offices and will have an easier time staying afloat. You could even charge more for rent if the economy is growing and businesses are being successful. However, it might be harder for you to fill a building like this if the economy is struggling or is not moving along as well as it should.

Whatever the case might be, you will have to be aware of how the economy is changing and what the demand for an office property might be. There is always a chance that an office building might be a more worthwhile investment based on the availability of suitable renters. A property that attracts more tenants will be not only profitable, but also a little more valuable. The overall potential for the property to keep growing in value could be great.

Industrial Properties

Some properties are designed with more specialized needs in mind. These are known as industrial properties. Industrial property is generally used for producing items, storing and repairing, and offering services to other industries.

Industrial properties include:

- Factories to produce items for sale to the public. These include machines, materials, and useful items of every description.

- Distribution centers where items can be sent out to other business sites.

- Storage centers to offer safe spaces where people can secure assets or resources. Some storage sites focus on cold storage.

- Power-generating functions. These include places that operate nuclear reactors, wind turbines, electricity, and other utilities.

- Garages to store vehicles and to do repairs and maintenance.

Industrial properties are attractive as they can be developed to house different facilities.

You would have to be aware of what the property is being used for and if there is future potential that could increase the value.

Look at how the property is being maintained and that it is not an eye-sore in the community.

Understand the environmental impact that some industrial properties cause. An industrial site that pollutes the air or negatively impacts soil conditions might not be worth as much money due to the problems it could produce. Sometimes the individual tenant is the major factor, but in other cases, it is what takes place on the property itself.

The options you have for properties you might wish to invest in are vast and should be explored. Investigate different properties to see which ones could work for your investment needs and those you know are useful and ideal.

Chapter 4: What to Consider Before You Invest In Real Estate

Real estate is always evolving with new things and ideas to explore. There are no limits to what types of properties you could invest in and turn your investment into a money-making proposition. The thrill of investing in real estate is unlike anything else you might experience.

The risks of entering into the real estate market can be high. You do not want to risk buying a property without knowing what you can do with it. You have to be aware of how the market can change while recognizing the financial concerns that often come with fluctuations in the economy.

You will have to be cautious when looking at what you can get out of your investment. The potential to make money is there and you have to protect your investment and know what your investment can buy and realistically what the returns can be.

Review Your Mindset

The real estate world is vast and complex and is composed of many types of properties that you could work with. Real estate can be challenging and a tough market. This investment option will be long-term to reap benefits. It will require keeping the property maintained and finding enough tenants and the right tenants. This will take a lot of effort on your part and it will not always be easy. You need a good mindset that can handle the effort required to keep a property valuable.

You might have to hold onto a property for years. Real estate is something that does not change in value overnight. As the owner of a property, you would have to see to the maintenance, that it is protected and safe, and that the tenants are appropriately protected.

The financial and analytical aspects of investing can be difficult and time-consuming. Only those with a strong mindset and ability to handle the complexities that come with investing in real estate can succeed in this field. You have to be able to handle looking after the property and be mentally able to meet the challenge as well as understanding the market. You have to do the research and conduct a full analysis of your finances.

Be prepared as this is a field that is very detailed and complex. Investing can be great if you know what you are doing, but it can also be a nightmare if you are not prepared.

You might not utilize the property you invest in. You might not live in it or have any use for its general features. This is definitely the case for many commercial or industrial properties. You will have to make decisions about how the property can be used and who will use it. Do not let your personal needs or thoughts get in the way. Keep your mindset clear and free from any thoughts you might have over how you will use the property yourself. Look more into what will happen in the future and how your property will change over time.

Watch Your Emotions

You might begin to develop some emotions relating to whatever you are investing in. You might feel overly attached to a certain property. There is nothing wrong with feeling proud about the work that you might have done on a certain property. We all have our own feelings that guide us through our lives. There are times when emotions can get in the way. When investing, you might become so attached to something that you do not want to sell it even when the market suggests that you need to sell it now or risk suffering a sizable loss.

Keep your emotions in check while investing. Do not get emotionally attached to a property you own. That emotion could cloud your thinking and keep you from being rational. You might make poor decisions relating to the properties you own or want to work with as a result.

Review Many Properties

Very few investments are quite as diverse as real estate. From terraced houses to industrial warehouse buildings, you could invest in practically any kind of building. Do not buy the first one that stands out right away. You will have to review many properties to get an idea of what is available and what you can benefit from the most.

You could find some properties that are increasing in value thanks to changes in a local market. Others might be declining due to being in disrepair. Whatever the case is, there is always a reason why a property is listed at a certain value. Look into each property you find and find something you are comfortable with to use your funds.

Do not just jump into the first investment that you think is worthwhile. The odds are there might be something else that could be even more valuable or useful. Maybe that alternative option is just down the street. Be careful and caution and look into many options.

What Income Do You Wish to Generate?

Anyone can make money by investing in real estate. Those people who are focused and understand what they want to do will be more successful. Consider your plans for investing and what you want to do with them. In particular, you have to think about the income that you want to generate and how you will go about making it all work for you.

It is true that you could make money by selling your investment at a profit, but it could take years for you to do that. You could always make plans to do something more with your property if you want to get that money sooner.

You can always generate income without having to sell. You could get that extra money by renting to tenants or something you could add, install, or incorporate into the property. Consider other options or uses for your property to increase the revenue.

What Expenses?

The expenses associated with operating a real estate property can be high. You would not only have to pay for the value of the actual property but also regular charges relating to the following:

- Loan interest.

- Repairs or maintenance costs associated with the property.

- Regular fees to homeowners associations and other groups if applicable.

- Utilities.

- Insurance.

Each property has its own unique expenses. Some places that are larger in size and cater to more people might have larger expenses. Other sites might require more extensive repairs. Be sure you investigate all the costs involved so that you have a good idea of what you will spend on the property. The cost of the real estate might be high, but the cost for upkeep will increase the expenses.

Inflation Considerations

Inflation is a natural part of any economy. The cost of living is always going to keep on increasing. Inflation could be a good thing in the real estate market.

Real estate is an option to use to hedge against the rise of inflation. This is a major benefit when compared with other investment options. As inflation increases, the value of your real estate will also increase. The value is tied to the cost of various raw materials. Some of those materials may include ones that were used in the construction of a property. The increase in salaries that people earn might also have a slight impact on what you are investing in.

Inflation will easily cause the value of your real estate to increase over time. There is always the potential that the inflation rate or the cost of living might decrease. You need to compare the change in your home's value with the inflation rate to see what is changing with your property.

The United States Bureau of Labor Statistics states that the rate of inflation at the end of 2017 was around 2.1%. In June 2017, the rate was 1.6%. That same year in February, the rate was at 2.7%.

There is always a chance for the inflation rate to be negative too. The inflation rate had been as low as -1% in early 2015, for instance.

Inflation has been relatively consistent since the mid-1980s. The inflation rate has hardly been over 3 or 4 percent in value since then. Also, the potential for the inflation rate to really decline and drop is nowhere near as great it was in the early 20th Century. There were times in the early 1920s and early 1930s when the inflation rate was as low as -10%. With the economy being much more stable today, the potential for the inflation rate to really fall to that level today is minimal.

Tax Benefits

Property taxes are your next consideration. You will have to spend money on not only taxes based on the property's value but also taxes relating to other expenses associated with your property.

That does not mean all the taxes relating to your property will directly impact your life. You might be able to have some expenses relating to your property deducted from your income taxes. This reduces your overall tax burden if you are eligible.

The capital gains tax on your investment may also be deferred. This would occur after you sell the property. You may be able to defer having to spend money on that tax although the rules for the deferment will vary based on your situation. You would have to talk with a financial advisor or tax planner to see how this might work for you. Your situation will vary based on what you have and how the funds for your property are organized.

Additional information on taxes and how they may work for your investment will be covered later in this guide.

Your Financial History and Status

Have you taken a look at your credit score? This refers to how well you are able to manage your debts. Having a better credit score is vital for your investment. It may be easier for you to acquire real estate if you have a good score. This means that you will not be rejected for the purchase or a loan. Any loans you do take on would have fewer requirements. You might not have to spend as much money on the loan interest if you have a good credit score. Your down payment or other expenses may be reduced or even eliminated altogether.

People with better credit scores are often preferred by people who are trying to sell their properties too. A seller will often review the individual credit histories of people or other groups that want to acquire certain properties. When a seller sees that one entity has a good credit report, that seller will want to work with that person.

Check your credit score and if there are any issues associated with it. Whether it is an error on your report, a missing payment or even bankruptcy or other legal issue, you will have to get that concern cleared off of your record as soon as possible. It could take months or even years to clean your record depending on the situation. Whatever the case may be, you must keep the credit issues you have under control so you will not spend far too much money on your property.

You will need to talk to a credit repair specialist for help to get your credit history and status in a positive condition. Although it might take some time to have those issues resolved, it will be much easier for you to enter the real estate market if you have a strong credit rating. After all, it is much easier to get into real estate with a loan with a 3% interest rate than if you had poor credit and had a loan with a 6% rate (provided you were actually accepted to get a loan, that is).

How Much Control?

One great part of real estate investments is that you can control them in many ways. You can choose to have your property upgraded. You can add an extension to a building on your property or even repurpose it in some manner. Anything that you can do that is within your legal right based on the contract and property can make a difference. However, you should look at the total amount of control you have over your property before you start investing in it.

You may be able to upgrade or manage a property in different ways depending on the situation. It is essential to review the rules first. Some homeowners associations might disallow renovations and expansions, for instance. They might ask you to keep your property similar to others based on its architectural layout or the functions the property can support. Some other local government groups might prevent you from adding new utilities or connections to your property.

Sometimes you might not have a large enough share in investment to have control of how it operates. You might only own a small portion of the property. Maybe you are in a contract where you are not allowed to do certain things with the property.

Don't forget about the zoning laws relating to your property. You might only be able to do certain things based on the zone your building is in. This is especially true if you are trying to build a new home or office site in a certain area.

Look at the amount of control you will have for getting your investment to work for you. You might not be able to control anything in your property depending on the terms associated with the deal you have made.

Volatility and the Stock Market

Volatility is an important issue to consider. Volatility refers to how the value of the property can change quickly. Sometimes the value of your property might decline depending on what happens in the stock market. This was noticed in the 2000s when home values started to struggle as the stock market declined in value.

The potential for your home value to change quickly could be a threat to your investment plans. Watch how the market is changing and how it is evolving, so that you will have a clear idea of what to expect from your investment.

How Long Will You Hold It?

Some investments are made to be traded quickly. For instance, you might find stocks and commodities that you can buy and then sell in just a few days. Some trading services offer option trades where you can place an order to buy something at a certain price just a few hours or minutes after the order is placed. Many people work as day traders who execute several buy and sell trades each day. Everyone has their own ideas for how long he or she can hold onto their investments.

For real estate, you will have to hold onto your property for some time. It takes some time for the value of your property to change in value. You could buy and sell a property within the same calendar year, but it might not give you much of profit. If anything, the process of actually buying and selling the property and the costs associated with doing so might dissuade you from trying to sell it too soon. These include costs associated with any loans you take out and even an agent's services if you choose to hire a professional.

Be prepared to hold onto any real estate investment for a while. You might have to wait a few years before selling a property in order to make a noticeable profit provided it actually goes up in value. Of course, waiting a little longer to sell your property might actually be worthwhile when you consider the potential for the property's value to increase after some time with inflation often being a factor.

Real estate investing is not for the impatient. You will be in it for the long haul providing you have a good plan. Consider what you will do years from now.

How Long Should the Search Take?

Considering how extensive the real estate industry is, you should spend a good deal of time figuring out what property you want to invest in. It might take months for you to find the right property. You would have to do a lot of research to see what properties are available and what might be more inviting or interesting to you.

Sometimes your search will bring you to many markets. Every market is different from one another. You might find something across the street from where you are located. You could also find a property in another country. The search could be so extensive that you might consider markets that you never imagined you would enter.

You are going to spend a massive amount of money on one of these investments. The least you can do is search properties extensively so you can decide what makes a certain property more appropriate for your investment.

Look into many types of property to see what is suitable and useful. Whether it is specific kinds of residential properties or choices of different industries, you would have to research everything in your region to have a sensible idea of what is available and if it can be profitable for you.

It is easier for you to enjoy your investment and to get more out of your work if you are fully prepared, and to have a plan before you get started.

Chapter 5: How Much Money Is Required For Entering the Field?

The real question is how much money will you require? Be prepared to spend a decent amount of money to invest in real estate. The total will vary based on what property you choose.

The biggest concern about entering the real estate field is that these properties are very expensive when compared with other investment options. You could spend hundreds of thousands of dollars depending on what you decide to buy.

What Do Properties Cost?

There are some measuring sticks to get an idea of what you might spend on a property.

Zillow, a popular site devoted to reviewing real estate information, states that the median price of a home in the United States as of January 2018 is $256,000. Meanwhile, the median rental for apartments is around $1,600. In general, people can expect to spend about $140 to $170 per square foot on a typical property in the United States.

Marketwatch states that the cost of renting a square foot of office space will depend on the location. Marketwatch says that an office property in Atlanta costs around $20 per square foot as a rental. That total goes up to $35 per square foot in Chicago and even close to $70 per square foot in San Francisco. In other words, the cost of an office property will vary based on its size and where it is located.

It does not matter what you want to buy or where you will buy it; the cost will vary. This is why you need to do a lot of research to decide which investment is the right one for you.

An investment as valuable and potentially profitable and deciding on a purchase is something that you cannot afford to rush.

Review Property Values

The first thing you need to do is look into the values of properties that interest to you and compare it to others that are similar. You could always buy an entire property so you would have full control over the property or at least as many rights as possible depending on the contract.

You also have an option to buy just a small portion of a property too. You could acquire a few units of larger commercial building, for instance.

You must check on the value of a property based on location, demand, condition, size and many other factors that you will explore later on in this book. You have to be careful as sometimes a few factors might contribute to what makes a property thousands of dollars more in value than something similar in quality or size.

How Much Up Front?

You do not necessarily have to pay the entire price for a property up front. The high-value of the property makes it a challenge for many to pay for it completely. This is where loans and other financing plans come into play.

A great loan will help you enter the real estate market. A loan gives you access to funds that you need for the purchase. It is a simple investment that helps you cover the costs associated with the property. You can pay off that loan over time and even use any profits you make from rent or other income-generating conditions of your property to help to cover the costs associated with that loan. However, you still have to have the up-front money or the deposit.

You can always make a down payment to buy a property. This will work if you take out a loan for the balance of said property. The up-front payment particularly states that you are capable of paying for the property and that you will be ready to manage loan payments. The larger the deposit, the less loan you would have to arrange

The total value of the down payment will vary based on the size of the property and its listing value. You will spend about 20 percent of the value of the property on the down payment in most cases.

You do have the option to place a higher down payment. This might be worthwhile when you consider the reduced monthly payments and interest charges associated with a loan. But you must still have to have all that money arranged – the down payment and the loan pre-approved in order to make a reasonable offer that won't be rejected.

Can You Get a Property Without a Down Payment?

You always have the option to pay for a real estate property without having to have a down payment. Sellers are not very willing to entertain selling their property to people who might be struggling with their credit as they are not considered a good risk.

The added expense for a property without a down payment indicates the borrower is most likely a high-risk investor. Sellers prefer an investor who has money on hand. The last thing a banker wants to bear is a foreclosure on a property.

It is difficult to find real estate banker that would help you purchase a property without a down payment. These agencies are few and far between.

Any investment plans that do not include a down payment would entail huge interest rates. Sometimes the interest charges associated with that type of loan could make the investment far more expensive than is reasonable.

What is the Length of a Loan?

You must be prepared to spend a long time paying a loan for any real estate investment. A loan will include terms giving you the opportunity to pay off the loan over the course of a few years, sometimes with a penalty if you pay the loan before the amortization period (the length of time arranged to pay off your loan). Most real estate investment loans are for twenty or thirty years. Others may be for just ten years. The length of a loan is calculated according to what you have decided to pay per month.

Bankrate.com has an interest calculator that lets you determine the monthly payments and the interest charges you would incur during the life of your loan. This is all based on the amount of money of your loan (and does not include the down payment), the amortization period, and the annual interest rate.

Can You Pay It Off Early?

There are some cases where you might be able to pay off your real estate loan early. This is perfect if you want to sell something soon or if you have received enough income from that property to cover the entire loan. Some loans have a pre-payment clause where you can pay a loan down once a year or once every other year. There might be some early repayment fees that cost a certain percentage points of the loan. These fees are added to discourage people from retiring their loans too soon. Review the terms of your loan beforehand, so you understand the fees and other stipulations involved. This would help you to know if paying off the loan early is the right thing to do or not.

The Value of Leverage

Leverage is vital for helping you to enter into the real estate field. Leverage is utilized to help you get the best possible results when investing. In particular, you will show that you have the full capability of handling some kind of investment you might be considering.

In most cases, your leverage will come in the form of a loan. Loans have long been used for investment purposes. People often use loans to pay off massive expenses and can cover them over the course of years. This is convenient and useful, but it also entails interest charges as a means of covering the cost to arrange for the loan to be put in place. You have to make sure you are capable of paying it off. When used right, your loan will be the ideal leverage that you can use.

Leverage does not always have to involve a loan. You might have another property you own outright or another special investment outside of a loan that you might use. You could exchange your existing investment with the real estate dealer or banker to get the new property you want to buy. You could find many real estate service providers willing to take on various investments you have. You would have to talk to those dealers to see what they are willing to accept.

The leverage you use would still require a down payment just to show how committed you are to the transaction. That payment might be worth 20 percent or more of the property you are investing in.

Leverage can be risky. While it can help you get your foot in the investment door, it could still be problematic depending on what happens with your property in the future. There is always the risk that a property or other investment might lose value. This could make it where you could owe more money on your property than what it is actually worth.

Leverage can be valuable provided you understand how leverage works and what you expect to spend on your property.

What About A REIT?

One option you have for investing in real estate is to enter into a real estate investment trust or REIT. A trust operates as a company that holds real estate. It owns various types of real estate including homes and commercial properties. Many REITs operate office complexes, retail centers, warehouses, and many other properties.

People often enter into the real estate investing field by working with REITs. They know that by spending a small amount of money, they can enter into a trust and realize some of the profits from a property. This sounds like an appealing option, but that does not always mean it will be worthwhile.

To start, a person in a REIT might not have much say over how a property is chosen. That person would have to invest in the properties that the REIT operates and not in anything else. The investor would not have control over tenants, how rents are to be charged, and so forth. The investor might not have full access to all the profits and rewards that come with investment.

In short, a REIT has an interesting layout, but it will not give you much control. You need to fully understand what is involved in a REIT. Full information on a REIT and how it might work as an investment vehicle will be covered much later on in this book.

What About a Portion of a Property?

You also have the option to buy a portion of a larger property. You could buy one property in a terraced housing building; that is, you would own just one of the five or more houses that might be in that building. You could also acquire a few units in a commercial retail center or an office building.

This is an interesting way to invest in real estate as you will spend a smaller amount of money. You still have to be aware of the terms associated with doing so. You might not be allowed to modify a property as you see fit, for instance. Someone else might buy out whatever you own too. Any damages to one unit in a property might impact your unit as well; this could negatively hurt the value of what you own.

The total money you would spend will vary based on location. An investment like this is surely something that you should not take lightly.

Chapter 6: Should You Hire an Investment Agent?

Although finding real estate for sale can be a worthwhile endeavor, you have to look carefully at what is available on the market. It takes a while for you to figure out what the best property to invest in might be. The research you will go through is extensive and requires many steps.

Do you have to go through the whole process alone? You could use the services of someone who can assist you with many of the more complicated or technical aspects of real estate. As appealing as the market can be, it is often tough to work through a transaction on your own.

One of the most important options you have when planning on investing in real estate is to get an agent to help you. An agent will assist you with finding a valuable and unique property that you want to invest in.

Getting an agent on board to assist you with your real estate search might be vital to your success. An agent will assist you in deciding what kind of property, what to do to get more out of your property, and finding a good deal. The support that you could get from an agent may be vital to your success in finding and acquiring the right property for the right price.

Note: Hiring an agent for any part of the investment process is completely optional. You can get someone to help you with managing many points relating to the transaction, but you always have the option to complete the deal on your own. Be advised that it costs money to work with an agent. The associated costs involved with services will be covered later in this chapter.

What Does an Agent Do?

A real estate agent is one of the most important people you could hire during the process of finding and buying a property. An agent is a person who will represent you as you look for a property. Such a person will help you to review a local market and to identify great market indicators. The work offered by an agent can make a real difference in your search.

An agent will give you access to information about many properties and can even help you compare properties. This is vital for when you need to find and compare multiple properties during your search. The process of finding a space is stressful enough as it is; you could get an agent to assist you to make your search easier.

The agent can also assist you with the negotiation process after you find a place to buy. This service helps you to get a good deal on the property you want to invest in. The negotiation would take place directly between the agent and the other party in the transaction. This could work in your favor if you are not experienced in negotiations, or you are unaware of what you can do to make the negotiation process a success.

Buyer's Agent

There are two types of real estate investment agents to look for. The first is the buyer's agent. This is a person who represents the buyer in the transaction. That person will look for a quality property based on the demands that the buyer has. The goal is to find the cheapest possible property, the best property, and the one with the most potential to grow in value.

A buyer's agent can help you find a property and present your offer to the seller. You could even gain access to a building that you wish to acquire through an agent. Your agent will arrange a viewing so that you can view the property in order to make a decision.

Seller's Agent

The second type of agent is the seller's agent. This is a person who helps sell a property and will try to get the best possible deal for the seller. The agent can also give advice to the seller for ways to increase the value of the property. Advertisements and other marketing tools will also be used by the agent to make a property visible to other agents and the public.

Seller's agents are often recommended because of how complicated a sale can be. A seller might struggle with trying to manage many things relating to a home sale including plans to get the property in the best condition possible.

A seller could use the agent's help during the sale process because a seller might need to sell the property due to financial struggles. The seller might also need to find a new property to live in. The emotional work of the sale could also be extensive if the seller is dealing with a deceased family member that owned the property or is dealing with bankruptcy or the threat of foreclosure. Having an agent could help the seller manage this stressful part of trying to sell a property and get the best price for it, regardless of the circumstances.

Both buyer's and seller's agents will contact each another during the sale process. The two must come to an appropriate agreement to ensure that a transaction can move forward and satisfy the seller and the buyer.

Certification

The agent should be fully certified. This means that person is licensed to act on your behalf and manage a transaction.

If you want to hire an agent, you would have to find someone who is experienced and understands everything about the real estate market. An agent who is not certified might give you uneducated and uninformed advice and even false information.

An agent must complete several steps to be eligible to offer services to you:

1. The agent must be a legal resident of the country in which the property you want to invest in located.

Such an agent will help you with finding a good property based on market trends and other events that might be taking place in a certain region.

2. The appropriate educational standards must be met.

The courses that a person must take to become an agent will vary in each state or country. These rules ensure that people are knowledgeable about real estate industry and how it works. These include the rules of real estate ethics.

An agent in Colorado must complete 162 credit hours of classes relating to real estate sales before taking the appropriate exams. A person in Idaho only needs 90 credit hours of classes. These classes are to be certified by a state's Real Estate Board and provided to people at continuing education centers; some online service providers might also offer courses.

3. After completing the proper educational courses, the agent must complete the proper exams to be licensed to offer real estate services in his or her state.

The exams are stringent and pass marks are high to ensure quality agents are eligible for licensing.

4. Regular continuing education standards must also be met.

These standards often allow a person to take upgrading classes over time. These added classes typically relate to new developments in the real estate field. A proper exam may also be required. Continuing education courses are often required every few years although that time frame will vary by location.

By completing the appropriate courses, a person can be certified to work as a real estate agent. This allows that person to help people with buying and selling investment properties. You should ask an agent about his or her certification and experience if you wish to hire an agent.

What Does It Cost?

Although the services of an investment agent can be useful, one reason why many people are reluctant to hire one is the cost associated with an agent's services. You will often have to spend about 5 to 8 percent of the total selling price of the property.

Suppose you find a property on the market worth $400,000. If you are buying the property, the seller pays your agent a commission. That commission could be 3 to 6 percent of the selling price and it is paid by the seller. You, as the buyer, do not pay your agent any commission. You actually pay nothing to your real estate agent when he helps you buy a property. You pay commission to your agent when you sell a property.

You cannot negotiate the agent's cost when you are buying. You can, however, negotiate with the agent when he or she lists your property for sale. The commission is paid to your agent by you from the proceeds of your sale.

Should You Hire an Agent?

The odds are you might not be all that interested in hiring an agent for your investment needs. After all, you might want to do your own research so you could have more control over the process of finding a property.

After a while, the process of trying to find a property might become a hassle. You might get lost in all the work you are putting in. You could also struggle with trying to find a good investment that fits your needs. Having an agent to help you with the process might help if you are really having a tough time with the process.

You might not actually need to get an agent. You might have enough control over the process of finding a property. You could potentially understand all the ins and outs of whatever you want to enter into.

Of course, the cost associated with an agent might be a burden to bear with. Having to spend all that extra money on getting a property ready for an agent's services can be a hassle.

In the end, you should decide for yourself whether or not you want to get an agent to help you out. Having an agent could work if you really need the extra help with getting a property for your investment, but the cost involved could be a real problem. Think for yourself when getting into any investment as to whether or not an agent's services are necessary or if you feel you are better off not working with someone like this.

Chapter 7: Investing in Residential Properties

Our homes are important. It is in your home that everything important in your life will take place. It is where your family grows up and where great memories are made. Every room in a home will have its own special meaning.

People are willing to pay top dollar for the best possible homes. They want places that they know are perfect for their lives. People want to live not too far from their places of work or near schools for the children. They also want homes where they can enjoy all the activities they want to do. These include homes that can house many vehicles or even places that can be used to store bikes and sports equipment or a room for a bar or a place for a pool table or piano.

There is more to a home than just the functional use. Future homeowners want homes that they can feel comfortable with. They want to live in places they can love and cherish for generations to come. After all, a large investment like this is not something that should be taken lightly.

This all leads to the first type of property that you will learn about investing in. The residential property is one that could be worth hundreds of thousands of dollars. It might seem expensive, but it is an investment that is well worth the money spent.

You will be dealing with a property that could be very profitable. The potential for you to make money from a residential property is very strong because it is a necessity for so many people and the need is always there.

Types of Residential Properties

One of the best parts of investing in residential properties is that you can find many options in today's market. You can invest in a property that includes some special features. Some of these properties are built with specific types of people in mind. Others are made with certain physical features that make them different.

Here are a few of the more popular choices you can work with when finding a residential property. Each is unique.

Single-Family Home

A single-family home is a detached home that is built on a single lot. It typically has a garage that is either attached or detached from the home. This is a basic type of home that is attractive for investment because it offers a single space for living for a single-family. It is a residential property that there will always be a demand for, thus making it a popular investment choice.

A single-family home is a reliable investment option because it often has a better resale value. You could also renovate or restore the home in any way you see fit provided it meets local governmental standards. The privacy that comes with such a home makes it a popular choice for investing. A big plus is the fact that people will have a need for such properties no matter what the market is.

However, such a home can be hard to maintain. It can be difficult to keep the property in the best condition possible. A homeowner is responsible for all the utility charges associated with the home. The building guidelines of municipalities and local governments dictate how a home is to be maintained, what the buildings can be used for, and how the exteriors must look among other standards.

This type of home is still the most popular investment option in the market. Single-family homes are popular because they have many. You will rarely come across many homes that are exactly alike on the same street.

Condominiums

Not all people need or want a single-family home. Some people might not have a need for a private dwelling or a need for a yard. There are also cases when people might not be able to afford the cost of a home and need to live in a place that has cheaper monthly payments. This is where the condo building comes into play.

Condominiums are popular investments as they allow you to collect money from many people. A condo building includes many apartments, suites, or flats in a single building. It may come with community features like a fitness room, an exercise room, a laundry room, and a meeting space for local events.

If the condo owner owns the entire building, he does not have to bear with the expense of running such a property alone. Everyone occupying a condo building will cover the costs associated with maintenance, utilities, and more. Tenants usually form a committee to have as say in what happens within the property and can approach the owner if something needs to be addressed. Some condos will even use shared resources like access to the same power grid, certain landscaping services, and even the same television service provider that covers all the apartments in the property.

Depending on the property, you would also have to enforce specific rules to ensure that people do not renovate their individual units. There has to be uniformity within the building. There is also the need to ensure that all tenants in the same building are living in accordance with the standards you want them all to follow. These include rules for keeping their properties clean but also for being good neighbors who will not be threatening or bothersome to anyone else in the building. Being a good landlord will be covered later.

You might also have to hire a property management team to help you with maintenance, finding renters, having vacant apartments cleaned and repaired, and collecting the rents and damage deposits. This might be vital for ensuring the people who rent your investment property will feel as though they made the right choice. More importantly, they will know that you care about the property. More details on a property management team will also be listed later in this guide.

Condo buildings can include different sized units. These include smaller units for single people or slightly larger spaces for couples and still larger for groups of three or four people. The cost to of the rental will vary based on how large it is and how many features it has. Every condo building is unique and you will have to take everything into account when deciding on the type of building to invest in.

Townhouse

A townhouse is between a single home and a condo. Generally, each townhouse has three floors – basement, living area, and bedrooms/bathrooms on the top floor. There may be 4 townhouses connected by a series of shared walls between units. This would involve multiple people or families living in the same building. The living units are larger in size than what a condo building offers, but they are still smaller than that of a single-family home. If you purchase the entire building, this can be an attractive choice for investing because it can provide many tenants and separate living areas.

However, a townhome usually does not have shared amenities a condo building offers. A local neighborhood association might offer a community pool or meeting center in an area away from the townhomes, but that is not always the case. Also, while there is a sense of privacy with each unit separate from one another, that privacy is not always guaranteed because the grounds are shared.

Many townhomes might have slightly higher rents because of the larger units.

Terraced Houses

Terraced houses are larger rows of houses. That is, they are multiple homes laid out side-by-side. Each unit in the same building can be as large of a single-family home.

Investing in a terraced house is great as you can collect rent from many people. A terraced house will not cost as much to live in as a single home, thus making it more attractive to families. You have the option to purchase one or more units within the same terraced housing.

Similar to a condo or townhome, you would have to keep the maintenance standards for a terraced house consistent with all the other units. You have to use the same materials for renovating and maintaining each unit. Such houses might not have shared features like pools or common yards. There will be restrictions in additions or changing the looks of the exterior.

Farm or Ranch

Although it is not necessarily considered to be a residential property, a farm or ranch does have some features worth looking into. A farm or ranch is a larger land area with enough room for not only a home but also some farming buildings for storing vehicles and other farm equipment or livestock.

A property like this is more than just a place for someone to live. It is also a place where people can conduct a business. A farm could be used to raise animals for food production. It could also be used for growing crops, fruit, and vegetables.

The exciting thing about this is that a farm property could be developed and become more productive. It could have a few new buildings added too. These would help increase the value of land, thus making it all the more valuable among investment options.

There are rules and regulations about what can be done on a farm or ranch property. The land will be zoned to cover appropriate farming activities. It might be difficult to apply for more land for a growing farm without not only spending more money but also just trying to get that land zoned in your favor.

What Can You Do With Your Property?

Buying a residential property can be worthwhile and it will be an important investment in your life. You are not required to live in the property that you buy. You can always use the property as something that adds to the overall value of your portfolio.

Renovate the Property

One idea to consider for residential properties is renovating your home. There are many homes that need to be restored and refurbished. You might need to have a home rewired to work with modern electric functions. The plumbing might need to be upgraded. Maybe the heating and air conditioning system is out-of-date and needs to be replaced with something that uses less energy.

You can renovate a home to make it equal to today's standards. It could be restored with a new series of appliances, utility features, and accessibility points. It may also need landscaping or a different physical layout. Renovations could even entail repairing and replacing roofing, siding, windows, and any worn-out surfaces or materials in the home.

Renovations are perfect for making a home more livable and attractive. You will have to be careful to know how much you are willing to spend on the renovations. You might need some outside help for getting those renovations done. Plenty of planning is also required to figure out how long it will take to get everything completed and to decide the order each project or step in the process should be done.

Property Impacted by Foreclosures

A foreclosure is a situation where a person in forced to sell one's home to a bank or other lender. This is due to that person no longer being able to afford the home. The property is taken back by the bank at a loss, thus prompting the bank or another group to have to sell it at a cheaper rate.

The lender is willing to sell a foreclosed home at a cheaper rate. You might find a property that is about two-thirds of the value of what it was originally worth on the market. This is a great option for helping you to acquire a property at a discounted price. The lender will be willing to do make a deal just to try and recover some of the losses associated with that property.

In fact, you don't have to acquire a property specifically that has been foreclosed upon. You could save money by getting a property that is in an area impacted by foreclosures. Properties that haven't been foreclosed upon could lose value when others near them have been foreclosed upon. This is because the properties in that area become harder to promote. You could benefit by acquiring a property when the values are going down and then selling it when the foreclosures are resolved.

There's also the benefit that a property that was impacted by foreclosures but not directly foreclosed upon could be easier to maintain and operate. There is always the chance that a foreclosed property might not be in the best possible condition.

As you find a suitable property, you will have to watch for how well the region is recovering from foreclosures. It is easier for the values of homes to increase when the foreclosure rate starts to go down, and fewer homes are on the foreclosed block. You might not get a profit on the property if the foreclosure issue is not resolved anytime soon. You would have to avoid any spot that is bearing with an increase in foreclosures too, what with it possibly being harder for the property values to increase anytime soon in such a space.

How Does a Foreclosure Impact a Property's Value?

It is clear that buying a home in an area where foreclosures are common in is intriguing as a property like this could be cheaper and therefore likely to increase in value. Why would a home that hasn't been foreclosed upon lose value due to all the foreclosures nearby?

RealtyTrac estimates that a foreclosed home can lose about 20 to 30 percent of its value on the market. Meanwhile, a home about a quarter of a mile away from that foreclosed properly could lose 3 to 5 percent of its value.

The main reason for this is due to the appraisal process. An appraiser will review surrounding homes when determining what the value of a property should be. These homes, or comparables, are analyzed based on their values. A home could have its value adjusted to be on par with some of those comparables. When foreclosures take place, homes that are now vacant will become cheaper. This, in turn, creates a less valuable market, thus dragging down the prices of properties that are actually inhabited.

This is a problem that many homeowners struggle with. It is not something that they can control. The appraisers responsible for reviewing foreclosed properties are fully responsible for deciding the values, thus impacting the value of a home that hasn't been shuttered or left vacant. This makes it all the more important for you to find information on foreclosures wherever you are. Additional information on finding foreclosures will be listed later in this guide.

Rent Out Your Property

One option for investing in a property is to consider renting it out to other people. You can have someone live in your property and pay rent for as long as a person needs the property or for as long as it has been agreed upon. In many cases, you can simply operate as a landlord for someone who wants a home.

You can do this for any kind of property that you want to invest in. This could work if you have a single-family property in some nice are that would be suitable for vacation purposes. You can even do this in a home you live in yourself provided you are going to be out of the area for an extended period of time.

Short-term rentals can also work. Have you read about Airbnb and other home rental services? Such services make it easier for people to make money from renting out their homes by allowing people to live in their home for a period of time. A person could use your property for a few days at a time and have the amenities that might not be found in a traditional hotel and could be cheaper for them.

Review the Property Based on Functionality

Finding a great residential property to invest in is always worthwhile. You will have to consider the property's functionality. Choosing the right property should be based on how a property can be used and what your plans for it might be. You must look carefully at what you will get out of a property when you find something that you might want to invest in.

What Can Be Done With It?

Analyzing the property should start by taking a look at what can be done with it and how it can be used. Consider features like:

- How many rooms does the property have?

- How can the rooms be used?

- What are the utilities, appliances or other functional features

- Is there a garage? How many cars it can handle and how much storage space is available for other items?

A property that offers many things is always a good bet. It might be easier for you to make money from a property when you have something that is easy to use.

What Are the Zoning Rules?

Check on the zoning rules in the area that your property is located in. These include rules relating to what a property can be used for. A residential spot might be listed as a farm or ranch space where farming activities and large animals can be found in. Maybe it might be in a residential space that has limits for what types of on-property business endeavors can take place. These rules refer to what people can do from a business standpoint while in a residential space. Regardless of what the rules might be, you will have to watch for the important points relating to what you can get out of a property.

Who Can Live In the Property?

Some residential properties are better suited for certain types of people. This is a vital point to see when looking for a property that you want to rent out to others. A condo unit could be better suited to a single professional or maybe to a couple without children. A single-family home is best suited for a larger family with children and maybe more than two adults.

A property that can be used by more people will be more profitable. For an apartment building or terraced house, you could collect rent from many people if you owned the entire building. However, the cost of buying that property and the expenses needed for maintaining it might be too high depending on what you are planning. A larger property will incur more expenses, but there is always the chance that the rent would be a little higher.

The finances of the prospective renters has to also be considered. Some properties might cater to people who are affluent and want to rent a condo in an urban location near a large business district. A single-family home in a rural area might be less expensive to find and could cater toward families that need a quality home but a lower rent.

Be realistic when considering who might live in a property you are considering buying. The property should be considered based on what you feel is appropriate for its use at a time.

How Is the Market Growing?

Every real estate market is different based on how it is growing. Some markets might grow faster than others because they are in areas that are in demand.

The growth of a market is often measured by many factors:

- The number of days it takes for a home on the market to sell.

- The turnover rate of home sales; this refers to how long a person might hold onto a property for before selling it.

- How many homes are underwater; that is, a person owes more on a home than what it is worth.

- The foreclosure rate in a region.

- How the job growth rate in an area is changing.

- Whether the unemployment rate is rising or falling.

- The median credit score of people in a certain area.

- The population growth rate; this might influence how much of a demand there is for properties if the population is growing.

- Whatever might be opening in certain regions; a residential neighborhood might become popular if a few commercial sites open up nearby.

You should speak with a real estate agent to understand how a particular market of interest to you is growing. You might be steered toward another market depending on how a certain area is changing in value.

Factors That Influence the Value of a Property

While many things can impact the values of property in a market, there are even more specific points to look into when finding a property you might want to invest in. The value of a home can change rather quickly. There are many factors that will directly impact what the value of a property might be. You might be surprised at some of the factors that should be considered.

Size

The size of a property is important to consider. A larger property will be worth more than smaller properties. This is due to the added resources needed for building a home and maintaining it. A larger home has more rooms for storing items, thus making it easier for people to have more choices in how to utilize the property.

Plot of Land

Sometimes the plot of land that the property is built on could make an impact. The plot might be very large in size and could be conducive to more activities. You might have the option to add more buildings onto that plot of land. The plot of land will impact the home's value based more on how people might use or change a property.

A home might be more attractive because of how much room there is on the plot. A property with more area around it could be a little more private in nature. This could create a more inviting space. After all, everyone loves a little more room and some privacy. It would be no surprise that a property would be worth more because of the land it is on.

The rules for a plot of land could restrict what you can build. You might be allowed to build a new building or another structure on the land. The terms vary by location, but they are always worth investigating.

Layout

The layout of a property is important to understand as well. The layout is often organized based on the intended use of each room in a home. A place with more bathrooms and bedrooms often costs more to buy because it offers more areas for people to live in. The functionality of such rooms makes a property more valuable in general.

Sometimes the way individual bathrooms and bedrooms are laid out might make a great impact on a property's value. The features in a property need to be accessible and useful so everyone in the home can enjoy easy use. A home with fewer bedrooms could still be worth more if those individual bedrooms are larger. The home could be even more valuable if those bedrooms have ensuites.

Location

The location of a property could be a huge factor in its value. The location should be considered based on the following:

- A home is worth more if it is near a school, hospital, shopping, or a business center.

- A home on a quiet street is often worth more.

- The proximity of a home to highways is important. Some homes can be worth more if they are close to highways simply because of the convenience to get to work. This is not always the case as some homes might cost less if the highways nearby are busy. The noise factor could be an issue as well.

You might find some good locations that will influence the value of a property.

Foreclosures

Foreclosures will impact the values of houses in an area. This is due to home appraisers using base values of other properties to determine the values of all homes in an area. The number of foreclosures could keep your investment from being valuable. Then again, your investment could rise in value if you buy it while there are foreclosures on the market when they are resolved. Review the foreclosure rates in an area and trends associated with them.

Crime Concerns

Crime is a problem in many areas. This is especially the case with homes around urban areas that might not be patrolled well by the local police. A home in an area that has been plagued by crime might not be worth as much due to the security issues involved. You could always get an extensive security system, fencing, and other features added to protect a home. Even with that, those items might not necessarily increase the value of the home. Be aware of how crime might make an impact on the value of a home.

The Condition of the Home

The home's condition is important to review. A home will be worth less money if it requires more repairs. The repairs could vary and might involve replacing old utility fixtures or having new floors and windows installed among other things. You would have to review three points regarding the condition of the home:

1. What the current value of the property is.

2. What it would cost for you to do the repairs needed to restore the home.

3. How much money your property could be worth after all the repairs are done. This might require research

on-property prices in an area that were actually renovated and repaired.

Market Sentiment

The market sentiment is important to review. This refers to the general attitude that investors have toward a market. The sentiment is often based on what people might notice within a market and how it is changing.

Like with any other investment field, the real estate market can be subject to changes in sentiment. People might start feeling bullish about the market if they notice that home sales are up and that more homes are being built. Meanwhile, they could be bearish if they see foreclosures going up or a decline in home values. The attitudes that investors have could trigger changes that might cause the values of properties to go up or down.

These attitudes can cause the demands for real estate to change, thus directly influencing their values. Check with how investors and analysts feel about the market.

The Power of Trees

You might not think that trees are important to the value of your residential property, but the truth is that trees can actually make a difference. Trees, particularly mature ones, will help improve the value of your home.

People love properties that are carefully manicured. These include places with elaborate and unique landscapes. Any area that has a carefully prepared lawn will be worth more money. This is thanks to the added curb appeal of the property. A home will already be impressive to a prospective buyer even before that person walks into the home.

The trees on the property have to be appropriate. There are many things relating to trees that have to be considered:

- Mature trees that are taller and sturdier are appealing because people know they will be standing there and aren't going to be an obstruction.

- Trees must also be sturdy enough so as not to fall over or be at risk of causing damage to an area.

- Trees can be worth more if they can naturally create a comfortable amount of shade where otherwise might get very hot during the summer season.

- Trees need to be in appropriate areas where they will not obstruct the view. They should not cover a home's windows or obstruct walkways and doorways.

- The roots should have grown to where they will not obstruct a driveway, landscape, utility line or another thing under the ground.

In short, mature trees are best to have on a property because they add to the overall attractiveness. If you do wish to add trees, be careful where you place them and that you know the potential for growth and the expected root system growth. This is to ensure you don't add trees that might be too hard to manage.

A professional landscaping company can always be contacted for assistance with suggestions about adding trees. You can also use that company if you have a tree that needs to be removed altogether.

Job Market

The job market in a local area can play a huge role in the value of a home. When the job market rises, homes are likely to increase in value. This is because more people will be attracted to come to a region to live and work. They will want to find homes that they know are suitable and useful.

People always want to find homes close to where they work. They are more interested in those areas because they do not want to travel too far to get to work. Some people might even prefer properties close enough to their work places where they could actually walk or ride a bicycle to work.

A good example of this can be found in a 2017 report from Zillow. The real estate analysis group found that in 2016, the average home value in the Dallas area went up by a little more than 10 percent. This was thanks to the strong job market and economy within that region. Meanwhile, the home values in Baltimore, a market that had a weak economy and job market, only saw its properties increase by around 4 percent in that same time period.

This suggests that a place that has more job opportunities will be more attractive to investors. For Dallas, homes are becoming valuable because people know more jobs are in that region. Meanwhile, the home values in Baltimore are just rising alongside inflation like with any other market.

Check with a market you want to invest in to see how the economy is changing and how jobs are being created. Look for news updates relating to major businesses opening in a certain area and see if they have been influencing the values of property. Be aware of how the housing market is working alongside the local economy and job market.

Investigate how the market is growing near a residential community. There is always the chance that a community might be growing in popularity because of the companies arriving and the physical business areas being created nearby.

These areas could make living in an area more desirable, thus causing the property values to increase.

The Potential for Natural Disasters

One of the greatest worries surrounding any property is how natural disasters could affect a property. There is always a chance that a serious disaster could develop. The worst part is that no one knows for certain when such an event could occur. There is no way these can be prevented either. For instance:

- Homes in the southeast are often subjected to flooding and severe winds during the tropical storm season. Homes in Florida. Atlanta, New Orleans, and Houston could be harmed by hurricanes and tropical storms. Properties in the northeast and even eastern Canada could be impacted by the remnants of such storms.

- Earthquakes can happen in many parts of the western United States. This is especially true in California, a state that is right along a series of fault lines.

- Tornadoes can develop in the central part of the United States. These massive wind storms can develop in Missouri, Oklahoma, Kansas, and many other regions.

- Sinkholes can develop in some regions where the soil is soft and could cause the ground above it to collapse. Such holes are more likely to develop in Florida.

- Tidal waves, massive thunderstorms and even the natural erosion of the shoreline could hurt properties on coastal surfaces. These include coastal surfaces in California, Oregon, and both Carolinas.

Of course, natural disasters can occur in any part of the world. However, the areas listed above are more likely to experience them. The value of a home could decline if its location is prone to such disasters or has been deemed to be a high-risk area.

The one thing about residential properties that should be mentioned is that they all make for some great investments. Choose what fits in perfectly with what you want to realize from owning a property.

Chapter 8: Foreclosed Residential Properties

One of the most common concerns surrounding any residential property is foreclosures. This means that a person who owned the property is unable to make regular payments or sell it for a price that would satisfy the mortgage. That person would have been required to leave the home and someone else, generally the mortgage holder, will have taken full control of it.

In a foreclosure, a lender will attempt to try and recover the debts that the homeowner has failed to pay and the lender can force the homeowner to sell the property. In other words, the home has now become collateral for the lender.

Foreclosures were prominent throughout much of the 2000s. This came as the real estate market crashed and values of properties declined. The crash caused homeowners to no longer afford their homes, thus prompting them to abandon them. This happens when the cash from a sale of a property cannot retire the mortgage because the home's worth has declined.

This chapter is not intended to ignore the plight of people who have had to face foreclosures on their homes. If anything, many of these people had to submit to foreclosure because they had no other option. They might have dealt with a job loss or a medical emergency among other concerns. There is always a sensible reason why a foreclosure happens.

In the end, foreclosures do happen. Today, you have the option to buy one of those foreclosures as an investment.

You can choose to acquire residential property by going into the foreclosure market. This could work well to give you a sizable profit over time provided you understand how it works and that you are aware of the risks associated with a foreclosure.

Why Would a Home Be Foreclosed Upon?

There are many good reasons why a home could be foreclosed upon:

- A person who owned a home might no longer have the money to cover mortgage payments. This could have been due to something significant like that person no longer has a job.

- That person might have broken some of the rules associated with a mortgage agreement.

- Maybe that person might have been in some kind of legal trouble and had to stop paying for the home as a result.

- A homeowner might have struggled with health issues. That person or someone else in the family could have become ill and health costs made it impossible for payments to be made on the mortgage.

- A person might have simply abandoned the property altogether and left it completely unoccupied.

A difficult part about all of this is that many people don't know how a foreclosure can negatively affect one's credit rating. What is even worse is that in many cases, the foreclosure is not necessarily the homeowner's fault. There might have been far too many things coming into play that kept a person from being able to pay the mortgage.

A foreclosure occurs when a person has been unable to pay off the mortgage. This causes the lender or mortgage holder to take legal action to take back the property and it might be difficult for that party to recover the funds associated with the original mortgage.

This could be worthwhile for you as an investor when everything is considered. You could benefit from the foreclosure by having a property that is available for much less than what it might have originally been worth. You have a chance to make a profit from your investment thanks to the lower amount you have to put up to entering the market.

You might want to ask a seller about what led to the foreclosure event for the property that you are interested in buying. You should know about this so you can get an idea of whether or not a property was neglected and how long it was vacant. You can use this to decide on plans for buying it and what you must spend on renovating or restoring the property.

What Can You Save?

The total amount of money you will save by finding a foreclosed property will vary based on where the property is, how healthy the market is, and the individual situation that led to the foreclosure. There is no real standard for how much money you would save by buying a foreclosure. The totals will always be different.

A good rule of thumb is to expect to pay about 20 to 30 percent less than what the property was originally worth. Every seller or bank will have its own standards for how much it will sell a foreclosed property. Check on the value of the property versus other foreclosures a seller or bank might have to offer and review the history and the condition of the property you want to buy.

The Three Stages of Foreclosures

An interesting part of foreclosures is that there are three particular stages for the process. You can acquire a property to invest in at any one of these three stages. Be advised that the process is different in each situation.

Pre-Foreclosure Stage

The first type of foreclosure is a pre-foreclosure. This is where a property is about to enter into foreclosure. The homeowner will not have suffered the most damage to his credit rating just yet as he still owns the home and not a lender or bank. You can buy a home at this point as the owner will transfer the deed to you at a price you and the owner have agreed upon.

A lender or banker will not have to get involved. You will arrange for your own mortgage to pay off the existing mortgage unless the existing mortgage can be assumed. You will take on the property and will cover the expenses relating to it. You could even allow the person who used to own the house to live in it provided that person pays rent to you.

Foreclosure Stage

The foreclosure stage occurs when a property is in default. A lender will start a lawsuit against the homeowner. The lender will argue that it should have control of the home again as the owner is not paying the debts of it. A third-party may review the property in question and then choose to place the home for sale on the auction block.

You could use this opportunity to acquire a property at auction for less than its original value. This process works like with any other auction as the highest bidder will get the full ownership of the property. You have to know the original value and the present condition of the property to know what you should be bidding. More information on auctions will be covered in a later chapter.

Sometimes you can still acquire the home directly from the seller during the foreclosure stage.

Post-Foreclosure Stage

The post-foreclosure stage is when a lender has taken full control of the property. In some cases, the property will have already gone through an auction process and might be held by someone who was the highest bidder. Either way, the original homeowner no longer has control over the property. You may make an offer with the person who holds the deed to the property at this point. Be advised that the home value might still decrease this juncture.

The Three Methods of Foreclosing

There are three ways a home can be foreclosed upon. Each of these ways is different based on how the courts handle the process. Methods vary by state. Each option will hold its own standards for how you can arrange the purchase.

Strict

A strict foreclosure is where a lender must get approval from a court to recover its property. This is to allow the lender to put the property up for sale again. The property, in this case, must be worth less than the overall mortgage balance. The homeowner will have a deadline to pay the debt. That owner will lose the property if he does not pay it off by the deadline. You can choose to buy it from the owner. You would have to ensure the money you pay covers the debts.

Non-Judicial

A non-judicial foreclosure occurs when a lender can foreclose on a property without the court having to approve. The foreclosure must occur according to the terms of the deed and trust involved. A homeowner should be given a proper notification as to when the property will be ceased. You can step in to acquire the property at this point, but the window of opportunity might be shorter than what the time allowed for a strict foreclosure.

Judicial

The third type of foreclosure is a judicial foreclosure. In this instance, the court is responsible to determine if a foreclosure can occur. The lender does not have much control in this case outside of filing a lawsuit to try and get the process to move forward. A homeowner will be given a court's notice to pay the debts within a time period.

You have one of two options at this point. You can either acquire the property from the homeowner or wait for a public auction to occur. A home that is not paid off and is then foreclosed upon will be sent to a public auction. A representative of the local court or sheriff's department will be responsible for running the auction.

All of these foreclosure types for residential properties are important to review. You can always save money on residential investments when you search through the foreclosure market. You must still look at what is available. You must also understand how the market changes. Check with the state government where you plan on buying a foreclosure to see what the terms of a foreclosure are and what the process of acquiring a foreclosed property is.

Review Foreclosure Statistics

As you have read, foreclosures can directly impact the values of properties in any region. Foreclosures can negatively influence the market in a local area. If you search online, you can find information on how foreclosures are developing in certain places.

Here is a simple process you can use for reviewing foreclosure statistics in an area:

1. Go to the RealtyTrac website at realtytrac.com.

RealtyTrac is a website that offers up-to-date information on real estate in the United States.

2. Go to the Foreclosure Trends section of the Stats and Trends menu.

3. Click on any state that you want to find foreclosure statistics.

4. Keep clicking on each part of a state. You will get more detailed information on foreclosures in certain regions.

The site offers information on foreclosures by county, city, and zip code. For instance, if you click on North Carolina, you can then click on Wake County to find information on foreclosures there. You can then click on the city of Raleigh and then search for foreclosures by zip code.

5. Review the information in your selected area relating to how foreclosures are happening.

The site has information on how many homes are in foreclosure. You can review how those stats have changed over the last couple of years. All this information should help you see if a market is weakening or if it is growing.

You can be as narrow or broad in your research as you want. Whatever you do, you have to look at how the foreclosure statistics in an area might be changing. The historical information surrounding foreclosures will vary based on the area.

How Have Home Values Changed Due to Foreclosures?

Don't forget to review how the prices in a local area have changed as a result of foreclosures. Foreclosures make it harder for properties to be valuable. To review prices and changes:

1. Go to Zillow.com/home-values.

Zillow is a popular website that was formed by a few Microsoft executives in 2006. It was established as a place to offer information on homes for sale around the country.

2. Go to the search bar at the top of the site and then enter in the region for which you want to get home values.

Be as specific as you can. Zillow does offer information on all markets around the country, but it works best if you know the exact area where you want to find that information.

3. Select the market for which you want to get information.

4. Review the statistics relating to how home values are changing.

The site has listings on how many homes are foreclosed, how values are changing, and so forth. You could compare this information with details on home values in other nearby areas.

This should help you get an idea of how foreclosures are influencing the market. A full analysis of how home values are changing can help you understand what is going on in a region and give you a clear idea of what to expect in that region.

How Can You Acquire a Foreclosed Property?

The process of buying a foreclosed property as your investment should be explored. Some of the steps associated with finding a foreclosure are different than the steps involved in a different property. Make sure you plan your purchase ahead of time and that you know what you can afford to purchase:

1. Check a multiple listing service or MLS for information on homes available for sale on the foreclosure market.

2. Contact the lender of the loan or mortgage on a home in the listing.

3. Hire a buyer's agent for help if you wish. This is optional.

4. Order a full inspection of the property. This is to see that the property is in decent condition or to find out how many and what repairs are required.

5. Review the needs that the property owner has.

The owner might have a need to pay a certain amount of money to a lender. Put this into consideration when deciding the amount you are willing to spend on the property.

6. Plan a negotiation between yourself, the owner, and lender.

Your buyer's agent may help you with getting the negotiation process to work in your favor.

7. After an agreement is made, you can close the sale.

You should now have full ownership of the property in question at this point.

Be Aware of the Risks

As appealing as it can be to acquire a foreclosed property, you have to watch for the risks associated with doing so. These risks can keep you from being able to get the most out of your investment of interest. Besides, a foreclosure is a property that has been associated with some trouble that could end up being significant. You must look carefully at what you are getting out of a property such as this.

The Condition of the Home

Although a foreclosed home is going to cost less money to get, you will have to be aware of its condition as you acquire it. The condition of the home might be weak due to the original owner not being able to handle the costs associated with keeping it in the best possible shape. The owner could have ignored some of the basic standards needed for maintaining a property and keeping it protected and comfortable.

A full inspection of a property should be held before you invest in it. You must look at the possible cost associated with fixing up the property. Reviewing how well the property is laid out and what it features is always critical to your success when investing in it.

The Owner Might Be Absent

There is always a chance that the owner will not appear during the negotiation process. That person might try to get out of the home as soon as possible. This is a frustrating issue that can hold up the overall process of buying the home.

This move could especially hurt the negotiation process. The owner might not be cooperative and could even insist that he or she is still the rightful owner of a property. The worst part is that the negotiation process could be hung up to the point where no one will listen to anything or take it seriously. In the end, you might not make any progress if the owner is not willing to cooperate.

Hidden Expenses

The owner of the property could be hiding some additional expenses that might be too difficult for you to manage. These include:

- Overdue property taxes.

- Old insurance costs; this is regardless of whether an insurance policy is active or has been canceled due to overdue costs.

- Old utility bills.

- Any liabilities surrounding legal cases involving the home.

- Liens that are in existence and could cause you to pay more money; title insurance can help with keeping such liens from being a threat.

You might be responsible for paying off those extra debts depending on what someone owes. Do as much research as possible into the home to see if any of these debts might exist.

It is possible for to find a great foreclosed property on the market to give yourself a better chance at making a profit. Make sure you have a good plan to find a property that is worthwhile.

Chapter 9: Rental Properties

Not all residential properties that you find on the real estate market are ones that you have to live in. You don't even have to own a property that requires a long-term tenant. Rather, you can buy a property that people can rent for brief periods of time. It could be something that a person will use for a week while on vacation or just for a few weeks or months while waiting for another home to be made ready.

Such a residential property that you can rent out to other people is simply known as a rental property. This is a popular type of investment that could provide you with a great profit depending on how well you are able to attract renters.

The Basics of a Rental Property

To understand why a rental property is an intriguing type of residential property to invest in, you should look at what makes such a place appealing. A rental property is a type of building that an investor owns. That person could choose to allow various people to occupy the property. The owner will receive payments from the tenants.

The tenants who want to use the rental property can use it for a determined period of time. Some people might use that property for a few days. Others might stay in for weeks or months at a time. There are no real limits or standards for how long someone has to be a renter of the property. It will depend on the agreement between the owner and the renter.

Think about what you might experience when take a vacation. You might enjoy a nice hotel, but maybe that hotel isn't what you would find in a full-size home. You might want to find a larger property to rent, possibly one that is cheaper than a hotel. Even more importantly, you might be interested in a place that is right in the middle of the action. This is where a rental property can come into play. It gives you access to an outstanding and interesting place without requiring you to use a hotel.

You can benefit from a rental property by buying it and renting it out to others. You will be surprised at how interested people might be in your property. The potential for profits is great provided you find a place that is easy to use and easy to rent.

Types of Rental Properties

A majority of rental properties are residential. Practically any kind of home could be used as a rental property. You could find traditional single-family homes or smaller apartments or condos for rent. Any home could be used as a rental property provided the person who owns it allows people to use it for brief periods of time.

Many of the more popular rental properties are larger vacation homes. These are places located in attractive tourist destinations that people love to visit throughout the year. For instance, areas around the Mediterranean Sea, the Caribbean Sea and even around various islands of Indonesia are used as rental properties. People can reserve these large homes near beaches and local communities for a week at a time. These homes can be prepared to support the interests that people have as they arrive at some of these exciting places.

Some rental properties may be used for commercial purposes too. For instance, a shopping mall might offer a few retail spaces that people can rent out for a few weeks at a time. These might be useful for retailers that focus on seasonal products. A group that offers Halloween or Christmas products might be open for about four to six weeks. That group can use a commercial rental property so it does not have to establish a long-term contract.

The main point is that rental properties can be found anywhere in the world. You will be impressed with how many different rental properties there are when you look online. Various online databases can provide you with information on all the properties that are available for sale, which you could use as a rental property.

Why Would People Use a Rental Property?

When you look at rental properties, you might begin to ask yourself a simple question: "This looks like any ordinary home. So why would someone want to rent this place?" The truth is that your property will be much more than anything you might imagine when you market it as a rental space.

There are many reasons why people are willing to use rental properties:

- Some people want to stay in a nice property similar to what other people might live in while on vacation. Vacation homes are often more appealing places for people to stay at than traditional hotels.

- Some might also need a place to live while waiting for a home to be made available to them. This might work for people who are planning on moving to new homes but have to wait because those homes are either occupied by someone who is moving out, or those homes are being newly built and haven't been fully constructed yet.

- Others need places to live in if their existing homes are undergoing extensive renovation or repairs. For instance, a person could use a rental home for a week or two if their existing home is undergoing an extensive termite removal project.

- People who need to be based out of an area for a long-term business trip could use rental properties too. These include people who might need to stay for a month and want to stay in a home rather than a hotel.

- Some people want to stay at places that offer more than what a traditional hotel offer. Hotel rooms can be rather cramped. The amenities in a hotel might not be anywhere near as diverse or enjoyable as what someone might find in a larger rental property. They would have access to a kitchen and laundry facilities.

There are many reasons why people might be interested in rental properties. It is true that such a property could work for vacation needs. Investing in such a place is a worthwhile endeavor thanks to how these properties are in such demand.

A Focus on Tourism

Tourism is one of the largest industries in the world. People love to travel all around the world to see things that they've never experienced before. They want to learn all about the world around them and live as the locals do. One way that tourists can really immerse themselves in a local area is by staying in a rental property.

Rental properties can be found anywhere in the world. You might find rental properties in many great places that attract tourists. These include condos near Times Square in New York, the downtown Loop in Chicago, or along the Strip in Las Vegas among other popular tourist destinations.

Some properties may also be found in countries like Ireland, Greece, India, or Thailand among other spots. These homes might be found near water or in some larger urban areas. A rental property in India might be located along the shores of the Bay of Bengal, for instance. A home in Ireland could be situated alongside a large hill not too far from an old castle site or a whiskey distillery. Whatever the case, some of these rental properties might be more intriguing to people than traditional hotels.

Why Would You Want to Rent Out a Property?

Now you know why people want to rent properties. Why would you want to rent it out yourself?

Renting out a property could be a worthwhile endeavor. Here are a few reasons why:

- A property will become an asset rather than a liability. This is thanks to the property generating a possible profit.

- You will remain in full control over your home while a tenant pays off your mortgage. You could choose to charge the monthly mortgage payment to someone as rent due.

- You still have the full right to live in that property you are renting out. That is, you could move back into the home if a tenant chooses to vacate.

- There is always the potential that you can get your property to be in demand from other potential renters. The added demand could help you to charge a little more for rent provided you are careful with the plan and that you are fair with your renters.

Having a rental property is something worth looking into. You will not only help other people with finding a property but also help yourself in the process. This is an exciting point for managing a property that you deserve to explore when finding something of value for any need in your life.

How Would It Be Maintained?

An interesting thing about a rental property is that it offers more amenities to a person who lives there. You have to make sure that those amenities are available, that it doesn't run out of bathroom materials, clean towels, kitchen items, and many other things. After all, a good promotion that many rental property owners make sure their property is fully stocked, clean, and ready for new renters.

It is a good idea to hire a property management company to help you with having the rental property to be responsible for cleaning the property and having it stocked appropriately.

A property management team will be discussed in detail in the landlord chapter later in this guide. The person who rents your property may reserve it for a brief period of time and will not have an open-ended reservation, thus making it all the more important for the property to be maintained and reviewed regularly.

Tax Considerations

The taxes for a rental property will depend on the area, city, or state. Every part of the world has its own rules for taxes. Some places in the world don't have any property taxes. These include Malta, Monaco, Fiji, the Seychelles, Turks and Caicos, the Cayman Islands, and the United Arab Emirates. These are all popular tourist destinations and are appealing places to consider for rental properties. Then again, the cost to get one of these properties set up and maintained might be extremely high, but that is another story.

Property taxes might be higher in some regions. Property taxes are extremely high in New Jersey and Illinois and could be even higher in urban areas like Newark or Chicago. Such taxes might be reasonable if you can regularly get tenants to rent a property.

Local or Long Distance?

Acquiring a property for rental purposes can be a worthwhile endeavor but you would have to consider how far away your property will be and how difficult it may be to keep it ready for people to stay in.

Additional information on choosing between local or long-distance investments will be covered in a later chapter. It is vital that you consider where the property is located and if it is in an area where people might be interested in using it. You might have an easier time renting out a property in busy area than in an out-of-the-way neighborhood that might not be in much demand.

You can always look for a property in a local area that might be interesting. This could include something like a house located near a college campus. It could be a place where a college student or a series of students might live for a few weeks or months at a time. You could also find a local property near a major downtown hub that might be valuable to people who want to enjoy a fun weekend in the city.

However, long-distance properties might be perfect if you want to target people visiting a popular tourist spot.

What About Individual Rooms?

You don't always have to make an entire property available for rent. You can choose to allow individual rooms to be made available for a special need.

You can rent out certain rooms for one of many needs:

- A large dining area can be rented out for special parties or receptions.

- A bedroom can be rented out for an overnight stay.

- A large office area could be used for business events. These include conferences and other types of meetings.

- A garage could even be used for temporary vehicle storage.

Any room in a single property can be rented out and used by others. When you consider doing this, you have to decide what people could realistically use the area for. You would have to use a sensible pricing plan and establish ground rules for what people can and cannot do within the area. The key is to use common sense when figuring out what can be done.

Vetting Is Important

Although you can easily find people to rent a property to, you must be cautious when choosing the right people. Use a proper vetting process for every person who wants to rent a property from you regardless of how long they will use it for or what portion of the property they want to use.

Some people might engage in illegal activities in a room on your property or even in the entire building or lot. The worst part of this is that you might be held liable in the event that someone engages in illegal activities in or on your property. This is a serious problem that could hurt your bottom line and make it difficult for you to rent to someone else. There are penalties for allowing people to do illegal things on your property and those penalties could result in fines or imprisonment.

You must review everyone who rents from you. It is up to you to make your own judgment for who you allow to rent from you. If you do not want to hand your property over to a property management professional, use a copy of a rental agreement which you can find online. Make sure that you ask for references and that you check the references to make sure they are legitimate. Make sure the prospective renter is employed or has a source of income. It is also recommended that you ask for post-dated checks for the rent and a damage deposit. Online you can also find a check-list to record the condition of the property for the renter to sign before the renter moves in. This check-list will be checked again with the renter when he or she vacates. If there is damage, the cost of the repairs will be deducted from the damage deposit you will be returning to them. This is just good business and no one should be insulted that you require this information.

Chapter 10: Investing in Commercial Properties

The world of property investing goes well beyond just traditional residential properties. You can also invest in some appealing commercial properties. These are places that house businesses and retail shops. You can make money if you own the entire building by charging rent to companies who wish to use the building or a portion of the building. You could also earn money from the increase in the value of your property. A fully rented commercial building is easier to sell than one that is vacant or only partially rented.

Commercial spaces are popular because they are versatile. You can find some places where people can shop for products and services. You can also look for properties where people can set up offices and places of operation. Some commercial properties might come as single-floor buildings that house basic workspaces. Others can be several stories and include enough room for many businesses.

An Investment Is Versatile

Commercial properties are popular for being available in many forms. You can invest in a few units in an office building or an entire floor. You could also invest in one retail unit in a spot. There is also the option to buy the entire physical building and collect rent from many tenants if you wish to go that route.

It is up to you to figure out how you will use your commercial investment. Think about how it will be laid out and what you can afford to spend money on when finding an investment of value. You will surely notice something that you will want to find in any situation you want to enter into.

Rentable and Usable Square Footage and How It Impacts the Value

The value of a commercial property is a little different from a residential building. A traditional home might have a value based on the number of rooms. For a commercial property, the valued is based on the rentable and usable square footage.

First, let's look at the usable square footage. The usable area of a property is the space that a tenant would actually occupy. This would include rooms for office cubicles or workstations, conference rooms and other rooms necessary for regular business functions. Even the hallways and bathrooms are included in the usable square footage.

The rentable square footage is what most commercial property values are based on. The features that are included in the rentable square footage include:

- Public lobbies.

- Public restrooms.

- Stairwells that lead to multiple spots.

- Shared hallways.

- Storage rooms.

Tenants in commercial buildings pay for a part of the shared space plus the usable space that they will have for their own business. The commercial property could offer areas for for more than one business in the building.

Here's a simple example of how a business might use a property and how it would pay its regular rent:

1. A business might buy the rights to use an entire floor of space in a large office building.

2. That business will pay for the usable square footage. This includes everything on that floor that the business will exclusively use.

3. The business will also have to pay a portion for the rentable square footage. This includes a lobby on the ground floor all the businesses in the building use.

4. The utilities and other charges that would be used by the business must also be paid for. These include energy and plumbing services. The charges will vary based on how many utilities are being used and they will pay for their own communication lines.

What About the Load Factor?

The load factor is the ratio between a load that one might use divided by the maximum load. For a commercial property, this is calculated by:

1. Take the rentable square feet.

2. Divide it by the usable square feet. The result is the load factor.

If a commercial building has 300,000 rentable square feet. It might contain about 20,000 square feet of shared space. Therefore, the property has 280,000 square feet of usable space.

To calculate the load factor for that property, divide 300,000 by 280,000. This gives you a load factor of 1.071. The total load factor percentage is 7.1%. In other words, only a very small amount of space in the commercial property would be shared among other businesses in the building.

This could be used when calculating the total rents. The business will pay for their own usable spaces, but they will also have to pay for the shared space. A place with a larger load factor will have a greater rent. In fact, a place that has more rentable square footage will cost more than usable square footage. Be aware of this when looking at the values of commercial properties and how much you could potentially charge businesses for rent.

How Long Is a Commercial Lease?

A commercial lease is generally longer than a residential lease. A lease is a document that lists the relationship between the property owner and the business or tenant. A lease should cover information on the length of the lease, the rent that is to be paid monthly, terms for repairs, renovations, and other factors that may be incorporated into an agreement.

A commercial lease is at least ten to twenty years in many cases. This ensures that a business will have an agreement to operate in one area for a long period of time. Having a longer lease ensures consistency and a guarantee for consistent payments.

Of course, there is a potential that a lease might be arranged for shorter time. A lease should include a condition for how the tenant can dissolve the lease. This might be vital if a business suddenly stops operating for some reason. A break clause is the most commonly used rule in this case. Such a clause would create an agreement for someone to break a lease provided a reasonable advance notice is provided.

Any contracts you establish with tenants should be reviewed appropriately. Your goal is to have a business stay in your building for as long as possible. However, you need a smart plan.

Offer a Property to Many Parties

One of the best parts of having a commercial property as an investment comes from how you can offer that property to multiple parties. You can choose to have many people rent individual areas within a building. Here are a few of the more common examples of how many people can use a commercial property:

- An office property can include many areas suitable for law firms, accounting firms, and other professional white collar groups that want to use the same building. Each individual group can reserve a portion of the building for their own private office needs.

- A shopping mall, strip mall, or other basic collection of retailers can include individual areas for retailers to operate their stores.

- Some other buildings may also include larger office workstations that may be shared by people from many businesses. These include massive areas where multiple groups can share the same meeting rooms, computer areas, and more. The tenants would share one large rental cost that covers the entire building.

No matter what businesses use your property of interest, you can be assured to receive a sensible income. You will not be reliant on just one person either. That is, you will not risk losing all your income if one person or a business vacates the property for any reason.

Be Aware of How Properties Are Managed

It is clear that commercial property can be a worthwhile investment if you have a good plan in mind for getting it ready and useful. You would have to be careful about how a property is being run.

Some tenants might spend more on rent if they occupy larger areas. A shopping mall would generate more rent from a massive anchor tenant like Macy's, Bloomingdale's, or Belk. That mall would be hit hard financially if one of those large tenants vacated. This can be seen as many malls were hurt by Sears' struggles as the company closed locations all around the United States and pulled out of Canada altogether.

A smaller vacancy might not be much of a problem. If a small mall kiosk that sold mobile phones closed, if would not affect your bottom line severely. You would have a bigger problem if a retailer like Foot Locker, H&M, Gamestop, or some other mid-sized tenant vacated. The financial damage could be even worse if a massive multi-story retailer left.

You will have to see how well tenants utilize a commercial property. There is always a chance that a property might work with many tenants that have their own individual company but want to use the same overall property.

What Drives the Popularity of Commercial Properties?

There are many things that can directly influence how popular a commercial real estate building is. Research your commercial investment options based on factors like the following points.

Location

The location of a commercial property is very important. You have to look at where the property is and its surrounding areas and how easy it is for people to access an area. A property located near a sizable residential area is always a good bet as people have easy access. It could also be perfect for people who are looking for jobs that are not too far from home.

The visibility of that location is important too. For instance, a commercial property located near a large highway will be easier for people to notice, thus adding to its recognition.

How Unique the Space Is

A location could become popular if you think about how unique that location. Some commercial properties might be intriguing based on the square footage available, how many tenants can be accommodated, and even the architectural features.

An area that is too commonplace might be worth less. A regular strip mall could be just ordinary and might not have high rents. Be careful so you don't buy a property that is not interesting and attractive.

Population Surrounding the Area

The population around a commercial building is important to analyze. Commercial properties are more valuable when the population density is greater. This means there are more people in an area that might actually make use of the commercial building. This, in turn, causes the value of the property to increase because the potential customer pool is larger.

The population growth in an area can also be a factor. A market that is growing in size could be a more viable place for people to do business. This is thanks to the increased potential for more people to go shopping or to look for services.

When the population in an area expands, there is a potential for more businesses to congregate. It might be tougher for some businesses to find clients due to the added competition that comes with growth. Business properties might actually be worth more if the supply is less than the demand in a region.

The growth rate of a property's value might shrink if the demand is being met as the population increases.

The Condition of the Property

As with a residential building, the condition of a commercial property can make a real difference. A commercial property needs to be carefully maintained and in good repair for it to be useful or valuable. You always have the option to buy and restore a commercial property before making it available for rent. You could even renovate it to create new floor plans that to accommodate the needs of specific types of businesses.

The Type of Business a Property Is Suited For

Some commercial properties are better suited for certain types of businesses. For instance, you might find a larger single-tenant property that could be useful for a supermarket or another retailer. A strip mall might offer good areas for small dining establishments or specialty fashion boutiques.

There might also be some commercial properties that focus on professional businesses. These include dental offices, legal firms, insurance brokers, travel agents, and real estate offices etc. You have to look at how the site might be suitable for certain businesses and not others.

Income Levels in an Area

The income levels of people in a region should be considered carefully. It might be easier for a commercial property to have a greater value if the income levels of the population in a local area are higher. People who make more money are more likely to use the services that certain commercial spaces might offer. Sometimes the companies that can pay those salaries might be likely to afford the higher rents.

Of course, the income levels might be reflected in the properties located near a commercial site. A place with more valuable homes could have commercial properties that are also valuable and could increase the total costs. It only makes sense that people would pay more for commercial rent where they can afford expensive houses. Do your research and analysis of what is available when looking for a property of value to invest in.

Other Important Factors

There are many additional factors that need to be explored when looking for a commercial property:

- The cyclical demand for a property can change over time.

- The potential for a business site to be improved upon or renovated.

- The competition from other businesses in the area.

- Zoning rules relating to the use of a property.

- Demographics relating to what is in an area.

- How much traffic might the businesses attract.

Review the Motivation

To managing real estate one should understand the motivation that people have for working in a particular property. A start-up might be trying to get off of the ground. It might want to rent a property that is cheap to rent. The start-up will need to conserve its money by working in a place that is not too flashy. It might be willing to choose an older property. That new business can always move to a more modern place down the road once it becomes established.

Some people have a need for high-tech materials and they might be willing to spend extra to rent a property that will support more technical functions.

Others might want to rent open areas that they can be creative in. This is definitely the case with open workspaces and creative sites where groups can work in the same area and share equipment and material.

You can find many commercial properties that serve the needs of various people. Not all people are willing to spend lots of money for rent. You have to look at what types of people would use the commercial property and why they want to use it. This gives you an idea of the clientele that you can expect to find plus how much those people might be willing to spend.

You will be impressed with the many commercial properties that are available for you to consider. Look at how the property is already occupied, what rents can be generated, and how it might be utilized.

Chapter 11: Types of Commercial Properties – What Works For You?

Various commercial properties are designed with specific intentions. That is, some buildings might be better suited for certain types of businesses that cater to specific groups of people.

The variety of commercial properties on the market is one of the more intriguing aspects of investing in them. Understanding the different kinds of properties will help you get a better idea of what you should be investing in and what to expect in revenue.

Retail

The most popular type of investment is in the retail sector. Retail property is a basic type of property that offers shopping opportunities for people. Commonplace retail properties include shopping malls, supermarkets, fashion boutiques, hairdressers, barbershops, shoe stores, etc. These are types of businesses that offer something special to individual customers.

Retail space can be large or small. You could invest in one that caters to one business, or choose a much larger option that houses several retailers. Sometimes you might find a retail investment where one anchor unit is larger than several others. For instance, a supermarket might anchor a strip mall featuring many other smaller businesses.

Office

An office property is a building that focuses on specific business functions. Instead of offering retail services, an office may include more professional businesses like legal or accounting firms or insurance agencies among others.

Office properties can be found in many places. You can find them in massive downtown buildings or in smaller professional buildings in suburban areas. Some single-tenant properties may also be available, although those office properties are few and far between. An office building will more than likely offer several areas for multiple businesses to work in.

Some buildings might focus on very specific types of businesses. You might find some tech-oriented office properties that concentrate on IT businesses. Maybe you could find a health park that houses businesses devoted to medical and health-related functions.

Leisure

A leisure-oriented business concentrates on entertainment functions. They are places for people who want some place to stay for the night, where they can get a good meal, or where they can find entertainment. Leisure business sites include restaurants and cafes, hotels, sporting facilities, and many other places. Such places are often housed in smaller buildings or places that are only dedicated to one function. The demand for such places can be rather high.

Healthcare

A healthcare business building is a place that concentrates on services relating to health needs and services. A hospital is a type of healthcare business. Some hospitals might specialize in certain services. These include services for surgical procedures, services for children, and so forth.

A healthcare business can be found in many forms. You can find many businesses that go well beyond a traditional hospital. These include:

- Urgent care centers.

- Vision care centers including laser eye surgical centers.

- Dental offices including orthodontic and cosmetic dental offices.

- Primary care centers or clinics for medical services not as intensive as a hospital.

- Senior care centers, such as nursing and assisted living homes.

- Rehabilitation centers for those who have experienced significant injuries or are trying to recover from drug or substance addictions.

Healthcare centers could be profitable over time. The demand is always going to be high for health-related services; everyone will experience some kind of health issue at some point in life. Investing in a place like this is a good option for your investment.

What Works for You?

All of these options for commercial properties are worth checking out. Not every type of property is right for you, and just because one particular market is thriving and growing does not mean it is the best one for you to enter into.

Maintenance

Look at the maintenance needs of a property. It might cost a bit of money to regularly maintain a business site due to the many people who use it.

An office property will generally require less maintenance. This is due to there being fewer people in an office at a given time. A retail or leisure space might have more people visiting at a given time. Maintenance will be greater because of all the extra traffic.

Hiring a property management team to help you with maintenance is vital to the success of your investment. Such a team will help you keep it in the best possible condition. They will also advise you when something needs replacement. You will learn more about the value of a property management team later in this guide.

Lease Length

The length of a lease may vary based on the type of property you invest in. An office lease might be for three to fifteen years. A larger business will have a longer term. A retail lease can be for five to twenty years depending on the size of the business. A larger retailer that takes up more space might choose to get an even longer lease depending on the viability of the location.

The overall length of the lease is important. Sometimes a property might be worth more if there is a good lease attached to it. When the lease is longer, the property value goes up thanks to the knowledge that someone will be in that property for a while. Sometimes it is the security that comes with knowing who will be in the property that can make all the difference when finding a good property to invest in.

What About Relocation?

Relocation is a concern that many people are often worried about. When a business relocates, it means the owner of the property has one less tenant to work with.

An office tenant is more likely to relocate than any other. Office tenants are easier to move because they don't have a lot of dedicated materials or equipment. There is always a chance for a business to contract or expand so that it has a specific need for a new office building. Sometimes a tenant might simply move somewhere with the belief that there is a better opportunity for that business based on what is happening in their sector or the location.

Retail, healthcare, and leisure properties are less likely to have relocation concerns. Such places are more likely to stay in one area. These businesses will have more complicated floor plans and heavier materials like surgical equipment, kitchen items, and other things that are not as easy to relocate.

Chapter 12: Industrial Properties

Now it is time to take about the third kind of property you can invest in – the industrial real estate property.

The concept of industrial property is technically a subsection of the commercial property field. Industrial buildings could be seen as being a part of its own individual class of buildings. Simply put, this new type of real estate is all about one thing – industrial purposes.

What Types of Industrial Properties Can You Invest In?

When you choose to invest in industrial property, you will have to think about managing it and how you are going to find people who might be interested in using it. You might even have to consider marketing the property based on some of the special features.

There are seven particular types you can consider.

Warehouses

A warehouse is a large building that focuses on storage. A place like this focuses heavily on securing materials or equipment. It could be used for storing minerals or other items that are needed for manufacturing or for public use. For instance, a warehouse might be a place that stores barrels of oil. The warehouse would secure those barrels so they can be transported to many different locations. The warehouse keeps the barrels protected from outside issues and can have added security monitoring to ensure that no one can enter the premises illegally.

You can market one of these investments by highlighting the use, security, convenience, organization, and management.

Cold Storage Buildings

Some warehouses are designed with refrigeration. A cold storage building is a property that has massive freezer spaces or cooling stations. A cold storage building is often used as a food distribution center. Some places may also be used for freezing medical items like vaccines or medicines that might be sensitive to warm or hot conditions. In fact, anything that needs to be kept chilled could use a cold storage building.

Look for cold storage buildings in warm climates. Those tend to be worth more because they are in greater demand. Even if the area has plenty of them, it could indicate the demand is high.

Garages

An industrial garage is designed not for private vehicles but rather for vehicles used for more intensive industrial or commercial needs. It may also house places for storing items relating to those vehicles.

An industrial garage could be used to store school buses. It can also house commercial aircraft if that garage is wide and tall enough. Some of these garages could also house farming vehicles or construction equipment. As long as the vehicle is designed with commercial or industrial intentions in mind, a garage can be used to secure it and to do repairs and maintenance.

Research and Development Facilities

Research and development, or R&D, is a vital industrial process. This refers to the analysis of different raw materials and how they can be used. R&D buildings can house large laboratories and offices where people work to review innovations and new products or services. Some of these buildings include their own dedicated manufacturing stations where the things they have developed can come to life.

R&D buildings are perfect for those in the electronics and computing industries, Biotech businesses, and healthcare to research products that might help the lives of people or to create new products.

Manufacturing Facilities

Manufacturing sites are among the more popular industrial places. These are areas that are more than just places for production; they also house massive machines that produce important products.

You will have to be cautious if you wish to invest in a property devoted to manufacturing. Such properties have large power generators and can require large amounts of energy. A manufacturing building may also require more ductwork, added air and water lines, and extensive ventilation and exhaust systems. Some specialized storage areas may also be needed in some of these places.

The amount of machinery needed in a manufacturing building will vary by client and the purpose. Some light manufacturing buildings make good investments as they use fewer utilities. These would be better suited for clothing manufacturers or other groups that don't require a lot of energy to produce certain products.

Distribution Centers

A distribution center is a place where people will send packages and other shipments to be redirected to another location.

Take the example of UPS, one of the top shipping service providers in the world. UPS has distribution centers all throughout the United States, Canada, and Mexico. Each of these places will receive packages that have to be shipped elsewhere. For instance, a person might ship a package through UPS out to Roswell, New Mexico. That package might go to a UPS distribution center in Albuquerque or El Paso, the two areas closest to Roswell.

A distribution center is an intriguing type of property to invest in thanks to how so many different businesses can use it. Whether it is a large business or a shipping company, you need to look at how well a tenant can use such a building. That business should be capable of using that center for an extended period.

Energy-Producing Spaces

Some industrial sites focus on producing energy. These include power plants of all kinds. Some sites include nuclear reactors or coal-burning plants. Others feature huge wind farms with massive windmills that collect energy. Even a huge solar array with panels scattered along a giant plot of land could be considered an industrial site.

Can an Office Be Included?

Some industrial properties will have offices within the facility. This would be a room of any size within the primary industrial area. Not every property will have an office, but it would help to have one. The value of a property might increase with an office included as it would be more functional.

The Three Sizes of Industrial Properties

There are three sizes of properties that you should review when looking for industrial property. These are terms that you will come across when looking for properties or when discussing your investment plans with someone who might help you find a suitable property to invest in.

Small

A smaller industrial site features a mix of office spaces and warehousing or manufacturing areas. It might be just one or two stories in size. A small site is prefect for mechanics or research labs. Start-up businesses can also use smaller sites. A place like this might have a greater turnover rate. The fact that start-up businesses often use these smaller spaces might make it more intriguing.

Large

A large property has storage or massive manufacturing equipment. It could be several stories in size and can hold more machines. Larger businesses can use these places for manufacturing, and distribution companies can also use these buildings for storing, sorting, and delivering items.

Big Box

A big box space is a much larger entity to invest in. A massive conglomerate like Amazon could use such a place as this.

A big box industrial site combines many functions into one location. It can hold products in a warehouse and then distribute them to many places including stores or directly to customers. It may have multiple storage units including regular and cold storage areas. Some manufacturing sites may also be included.

A business of the size of Amazon would surely benefit from a big box industrial site. It would host all the functions that the business has.

Industrial sites are exciting places to invest in. Businesses will often have a great need for these places to help them accommodate manufacturing, storing, and shipping. The potential for you to get something outstanding out of a property like this is something you need to look into.

Chapter 13: Analyzing Industrial Properties

Now that you know what types of industrial properties are available, you can spend some time looking into what makes certain places valuable.

How Is It Organized?

Every industrial property is organized with a certain function in mind. Some places are made to be shipping centers for moving items out to customers. Others are places where people make products and store them. Don't forget about research and development functions. There is always the chance that a property might have some office spaces inside too.

Be aware of the functionality. There are a few things you can do to check on the property:

1. Review the type of business that is situated on a property or any other businesses that have been situated there before.

2. If the property is new, look at the potential clients. Think about who might realistically use the property.

3. Analyze the needs that a client has for the property.

4. Review the spacing of the property, its floor plan, and how well it can support various machines and other devices.

5. Look at if it can be expanded.

You do have the option to reorganize an industrial site in any way that may be more profitable for you. You would have to spend an extra amount of money or a little more effort to get it organized in a way that you might prefer. You would have to contact a renovation or construction team to help you reorganize an industrial site too. The extensive technical features that are included in such a property might make it harder for you to reorganize as the wiring, ducts, and vents can be a real hassle.

Review the Size

Many industrial properties can be very large. While some smaller properties are available for start-ups, there are some massive buildings that may work for experienced businesses or those who provide specialized services.

The value of a property is often influenced by the usable square footage and the intention that a building is made for. A warehouse might not be worth as much as an R&D building due to how a warehouse is used simply for storage while an R&D building has more complicated requirements.

Utility Usage

The utilities used by an industrial site are vital to its success. There are many things that a site might require for its operation:

- The machines used within a business often require more energy than other devices. A site might put a significant drain on a local electric grid. Some industrial sites might have their own dedicated renewable power source fields or arrays, but that is optional and is not common.

- Ventilation is required to keep the inside of a property safe and easy for people to work and breathe. This is vital for when people are in contact with hazardous materials. Of course, proper ventilation is no substitute for general safety in the workplace.

- A massive heating and air conditioning system might be required for some buildings to keep the climate under control. This is especially the case for cold storage buildings.

- A generator is often required for some industrial buildings, especially for cold storage facilities. The generator has to keep the power on or else anything inside the property could be at risk of harm.

- Added water and sewage lines might be required due to the number of people using the property. These lines might work well for machines that use water in particular.

- Plenty of insulation is also needed to keep the inside of a building comfortable without any sudden changes in temperature. There must be adequate insulation if weather extremes are significant.

The cost of utilities and maintenance needs for an industrial site might be greater than some other place you can invest in. Be prepared to add this to your investment plans.

Added Insurance May Be Required

Insurance is a necessity for all real estate investments. It is even more important for an industrial property. A place like this can be pose risks to many people. Some hazards can develop and make a place a significant threat:

- Sometimes a machine in an industrial site might break down and cause injuries or go on fire.

- Exposure to loud noises, chemicals, and fumes can be prevalent in many industrial sites.

- Electrical materials could be exposed and can cause a shock risk to occupants or uses of electrical machinery.

- Places that need to be kept warm or cold can be dangerous to people who occupy the area for far too long. Any items that need to be protected from the heat or cold can also a threat of damage.

Although safety, prevention, and protection are all critical to keeping people safe, there will always be a risk of something hazardous happening in an industrial site. You will need to arrange adequate insurance.

The insurance policy you take out might have to be larger in value. This is to cover the expenses relating to any injuries that might take place, the values of any machines on a site, or even any possible material losses. A strong policy should have enough coverage for any losses that might take place at your facility.

Liability coverage is the most common type of policy you can arrange for an industrial property. Fire and flood coverage is a good idea as well, but liability coverage is critical for covering any injuries or other physical occurrences on a site. Even if you are not at the property, you might still be held liable for whatever happens.

Chapter 14: What About Bare Land?

Although it is great to buy real estate, you also have the choice to buy a bare plot of land. It could be a place where you would have the opportunity to build your own building according to the zoning and the rules for the area.

This sounds like an exciting endeavor. You could enjoy a little more freedom with your plot of land by planning a unique property.

Buying land is an interesting endeavor to consider. However, there is a potential that it could be more trouble than what it is worth. You have to investigate the permitted usage of any land purchases you are thinking about investing in.

About Land Purchases

Land use is determined by a local governing board. A local government determine what types of land can be made available for individual purchases. The government may have rules as to what can be built on land in a particular zone and have restrictions on how the buildings are to be used. Zoning will be discussed later in this guide.

Where Can the Land Be Found?

Land for sale is typically found in areas not too far from other properties. These include land that is located near residential communities or industrial sites. Some of these lands are zoned for specific purposes depending on what is located near it. You can visit a website like LandWatch to discover where you can find land. There are many places where land can be found for sale and the features of those areas will vary.

How Much Work Is Involved?

You have the option to create your own real estate on any plot of land you purchase. But it may take a lot of work, time, and money. The following are some steps to purchase your own plot of land:

1. You would have to review the location of the land.

The land should be located in an area not be too far away from utility services. It must also be near roads to where it will not be a challenge for you to access the property. In addition, the land must be sound and stable.

2. You must also review the zoning requirements for the property.

There might be limits as to what you can and cannot build. Zoning rules will be discussed later in this guide.

3. You must go through the process of acquire the land.

This process may be handled by a professional realtor. Some agents might specialize exclusively in land sales.

4. Count on a sizable amount of money to develop the property.

It can cost about $150 to $300 per square foot to build a building. You could expect to spend at least $200,000 on any building you wish to construct.

5. Proper utilities must be arranged to service your property.

Water and electric connections must be arranged. If your property is not connected to a municipal source, the water must be tested because sometimes the water in an area might not be potable.

6. The construction for the property must be carefully organized.

You will have to set up a construction plan based on the materials you need and the manpower you will hire. You might need to get a few outside contractors to help you. You will have to arrange for building permits, electrical permits, plumbing permits, and inspections.

7. Legal papers for your property will have to be filed as well.

Any new properties you have built would have to be reviewed and supported by a local government.

The process could take months to finish. It could be worthwhile if you consider the value of your property after the construction. You may wait years for the value to increase. As mentioned before, there is no guarantee that this would happen.

Buying land is a simple option to consider, but it should be compared with other possible real estate investments.

Chapter 15: Local or Long-Distance?

One of the best parts of investing in properties is that you have the right to invest in any kind of property you might want. You are not limited to just a local area near where you live.

It is true that you can find renters where you are located and have an easy time maintaining it. However, you could also consider some other place in the world. You might be impressed at how easy it is to buy a quality property anywhere. There might be a chance that a property you really want to invest in is located in some other part of the world that you might not have thought of.

As you invest, you must compare local and long-distance properties. Each option has its own positives and negatives worth exploring.

Local

You can choose to invest in a property in a local area. You will know more about the area in which your new property is located. You will be familiar with the rules surrounding the property, any taxes, or expenses you might have to pay, and so forth.

If you invest in a local area as a rental property, it will be easier for you to maintain as you can inspect the property regularly. You can head over to the place on occasion to see how well the property is being run and that it is always being stocked and maintained. You would have more control over this kind of property.

You could also save money by not having to hire a management company. It does take extra time to maintain the property properly and to inspect it on occasion.

The knowledge you have of a local area could be a benefit. You might not have to spend a lot of time finding a property because you know the area.

When to Choose a Local Property

You should choose to invest in a local property if:

- You understand all the aspects of your local market.

- You want more physical control over a property.

- You feel more comfortable with staying in a local area.

- Rental tenants might be easy to find.

- You wish to acquire other properties in the area; these include properties that might be near something you already own.

- The local market has good values associated with it, and you know what those costs are.

Long-Distance

You also have the option to purchase a long-distance property. You could choose to buy a property in a tourist destination or another place where the demand for rental properties might be very high.

You could do well with a long-distance property to offer for rent including around resort towns or popular tourist hubs. The potential for you to make a good income from your investment is high.

The big problem with a long-distance property is that you will not have much control over the property. Depending on its location, you might never actually visit the property. You could get videos or photos of it online while communicating with others regarding the property.

You would certainly have to contact a property management team to help you with having the rental property maintained, cleaned, rented to interested parties, and collecting the rent.

You might not be familiar with the laws and expenses that come with running a property in a certain region. You might have to do some extra to give you a clear idea of what to expect from your investment.

When to Invest In a Long-Distance Property

You can always invest in a long-distance property if:

- It is difficult to find a good property in the market where you live.

- The local market is not performing well.

- There is another market you know of that is really intriguing.

- You are looking to rent your property to tourists or other short-term groups.

- You want to find a commercial property that you know will attract tenants that will rent on a long-term basis.

- The values associated with properties long-distance are more conducive to your investment plans.

Chapter 16: Property Valuation

Now that you understand the many types of properties you can invest in, and what you need to consider, consider the value of a property you want to purchase.

The property valuation process is critical to your investment. It is also known as an appraisal process.

The process gives you an idea of whether or not the property you want to invest in is actually something you can afford. You need an appraisal done by a professional appraiser. Although some places might be profitable, there are never any guarantees that you will make money. Therefore, you have to look at the property value to see that it is something you could be comfortable with.

Reasons Why the Valuation Process Is Critical

The valuation or appraisal is designed to let you know what a property is worth. There are several additional reasons why this part of investing is critical:

- An appraisal is almost always required for the ownership of any real property to be transferred.

The process shows that you are serious about the transaction you want to enter into and that you really want to acquire the property.

- People use the values listed in the process to establish strategies for buying and selling.

The owner of a property might use the appraised value to determine the listing price. The value should be reasonable and relative to whatever the valuation suggests.

- The appraised value also determines how large a loan can be arranged from a lender.

The valuation makes it easier for lenders to understand the worth of a property, the amount of the mortgage that can be arranged and the down payment required to secure the property.

- Rent schedules and lease terms may be set based on what the appraisal.

- Negotiations might be easier when an estimated value is established.

- You can identify any hidden issues within your property through an appraisal.

Sometimes the appraisal will discover issues like mold, termite damage, lead paint, or other concerns. These are problems that might require you to make repairs. A home inspection combined with an appraisal will reveal problems that might deter you from completing the purchase. Sometimes the owner of a property will not be forthcoming with the issues of the property.

Hiring an Inspector

A home inspection is essential. An inspector will analyze the condition of the property. It is an extensive process that requires several steps for it to be as accurate as possible. A professional inspector should be hired to help you get a full review of your property.

The inspector must be someone who works on behalf of a bank or lender. The person must be fully trained in the field while offering a neutral approach to the inspection process.

There are a few things you should when hiring an inspector:

1. Check on the certifications that the inspector holds.

An inspector should be fully licensed to work in the field. You can review the United States National Registry website at asc.gov to get information on a person's registration and any licenses individuals hold. A license might be granted by the state where the property is located.

An inspector should be a member of a legitimate organization dedicated to appraisals. The Senior Real Property Appraiser and Member Appraisal Institute groups are the most prominent ones.

2. Talk with an inspector about his or her experience.

Ask the inspector his prior work. Talk about what that person has appraised in the past and how that person inspected certain properties.

Inspectors can work with multiple kinds of properties, but the best inspectors focus on just one particular type of property. Some focus on residential properties while others concentrate more on commercial spaces.

3. Review any references that the inspector has.

References list information on what an inspector has done. This includes details on how that person has worked for other people in the past.

4. Sign an agreement for the inspection.

The agreement states that you will work with the inspector and that you will pay for the inspection. The total value of the inspection might vary depending on the area, the size of the property, and the function of the property.

What Does the Inspection Cost?

The inspection costs can vary based on the property. Home Advisor estimates that you would spend about $300 to get a home inspected. That total could go up to $500 if you have a larger home. The total might be higher for a commercial or industrial property.

The amount of time needed to inspect the property could also make an impact on the cost. You might have to spend more if you have an older property.

The total will clearly be higher if the property is large. All inspectors have their own standards for what they will charge. You can always ask the inspector for a cost estimate at the beginning of the process.

The Inspection Process

The following steps are generally followed during the inspection:

1. The inspector will check the outside of the property.

The foundation, landscaping, and access points to the property will be analyzed. The construction of the property may also be reviewed to identify any problems.

2. The inside of the building can then be checked.

Each room must be inspected completely to determine how a property may be used.

3. All electrical features in the property are inspected to see that they are safe and are fully updated to modern certified standards.

4. The plumbing and HVAC systems are reviewed to see that everything is working appropriately.

5. The roof will be inspected to determine if the roofing material is adequate and in good repair.

6. The attic has to be inspected to determine the adequacy of the insulation and to look for any leakage and damage to rafters.

7. All windows and doors will be expected to determine leakage, damage, and if replacement is necessary.

Why Would a Valuation Be Low?

There might be times when a valuation might be lower than what you might have hoped. This could be a serious problem when you are trying to sell a property. Even more importantly, it could be an issue if your lender bases the amount they are willing to lend on the lower

There are many reasons why the overall valuation of your property might be low:

- The appraiser might think the area the property is situated in a depressed

  area, overlooks power lines or utility poles, an industrial area, or a gravel pit.

- The basement area may be sub-par or maybe there is no basement, just a crawl space or foundation.

- Appraisers might value individual things near a property differently from you.

Some appraisers might not consider a pool or tennis court a plus for your property and add it into the value.

- A market might be too hot. The prices might be rising so that those changes might not be reflected in the valuation of your property yet.

- Sometimes the appraiser's lack of experience might be a factor. Even a certified appraiser might not fully understand the true value of your property.

The general goal of the evaluation is to determine an accurate value for a property.

Chapter 17: Finding Hazardous Materials In a Property

There are often some hidden dangers that might be present in your property. The problem with investing in a property is that sometimes a prior owner might not tell you about any problems. Sometimes a person might not tell you about these issues out of fear that you will not buy the property because of those issues.

The truth is that you could increase the value if you fix those problems. Some concerns in a property might cause its value to drop, but when those issues are resolved, the value of the property will increase.

An inspector can help you to find various issues of a property so they can be taken care of properly. Hiring an inspector will help you identify problems and not only reduce the purchase cost of a property but also guide you toward what you should do to resolve such issues.

It might cost extra for you to ask for a hazardous material inspection. These inspections can be worthwhile when you consider how they can directly influence what you might get out of the valuation. You could also use these issues as leverage in negotiations as you attempt to have the owner resolve the issues or compensate you on the price.

Radon

Radon testing is important to identify one of the most harmful substances that could be in a property without anyone actually knowing it. This is a cancerous radioactive gas that could be found in any home. It is not easily identified because it is a colorless, odorless, and tasteless gas.

Radon is produced naturally by the breakdown of uranium in the earth's soil and rocks. The gas moves through the ground and into the air or into the foundation of a home. Sometimes the radon that naturally appears above the ground can seek into a home while the doors or windows are open. Radon may also enter the home through the water supply.

It might be easy for a home to collect radon as the foundation weakens.

A professional test can be used to identify radon in your home. The test may entail a review of water connections, the foundation of a property, and if the soil in an area is impacted by radon. This helps to determine how significant the radon problem might be. Sometimes the test will reveal that there is no radon, but it helps to complete the test anyway to be safe. It can cost around $100 to $200 to get such a test completed.

What About Reducing Radon Levels?

There are a few things that can be done to any property that might have radon. These can be done to protect a property and increase its value:

1. Seal off any cracks in the foundation. These include any holes that might have developed.

2. A sub-slab depressurization pipe may be installed. This uses a vent pipe that uses fans to prevent the gas from entering from outside the foundation.

3. Point-of-entry water filters that utilize granular activated carbon can help with protecting the water supply. This should be installed around plumbing fixtures and lines that enter the property.

The radon levels in a property should be tested again after the appropriate measures have been taken. This is to see that all changes in a property are adequate after the initial threat of radon is identified.

Asbestos

Asbestos is a dangerous concern that can be found in older properties. The use of asbestos has been outlawed in home construction projects in the United States since 1989. However, there are still some older homes that may still contain this dangerous material. Many properties outside the country might still have asbestos in them as each country has its own rules for managing asbestos.

Asbestos is a silicate mineral solution that is prepared in a series of thin fibers. These fibers had been used in many construction projects to absorb sound and to resist fires. These were used for insulation and to cover electrical wiring to keep them protected and secure.

Over time, it was determined that asbestos could be dangerous to people who are in contact with it. The small fibers that asbestos consists of can be easily inhaled. These could cause significant lung damage and may cause lung cancer, mesothelioma, or other severe illnesses. As a result, asbestos use has been eliminated throughout many countries. However, older properties may still contain some asbestos inside the walls or insulating surfaces.

You must order an asbestos check on your property of if it was constructed in the 1980s or earlier. This is especially the case if your property has a popcorn ceiling that was sprayed or painted on to hide imperfections with the natural ceiling surface.

Check and Removal Process

There are a few steps that have to be followed in the process of checking and removing asbestos. These are processes that must be handled by professional asbestos removers. Handling the process on your own could be extremely dangerous:

1. A professional should inspect floor and ceiling tiles, insulation around utilities, joint compounds, and pipe cement around the property.

2. Any suspected asbestos items should be taken to a laboratory to be analyzed. Microscopic reviews may help with finding any problems.

3. The actual removal process will require furniture, linen, and other items in the property to be removed. This is to keep those items from getting in touch with any asbestos fibers. The property should be empty or almost empty.

4. A humidifier should be added to the property to help facilitate the removal process. It is harder for asbestos fibers to move around when the air is damp.

5. Any tiles, cement materials or other items that contain asbestos will have to be chipped away and removed.

6. Vacuums are used to remove any asbestos fibers that might linger.

7. All surfaces where asbestos was found will have to be wiped down and cleaned thoroughly.

8. Another test may take place in a week or two. This is to ensure that the asbestos that had to be removed is actually gone.

9. Any insulation, cement or other materials that were removed should be replaced with new materials that do not contain asbestos.

Protective materials should be worn by those removing the asbestos and cleaning the area.

What Is the Cost?

Asbestos removal is critical to ensure your investment is protected and safe. The cost associated with removing this compound can be high:

- You could spend at least $400 on the asbestos testing process. The cost may be higher if the property is larger.

- The removal process can cost at least $2,000. It could get into the five-digit range if a large amount of asbestos is present.

- A follow-up inspection is needed to ensure all asbestos in a property has been removed. This will cost around $400 once again.

As mentioned earlier, you can always incorporate the cost of removing asbestos and testing it into the negotiation process for acquiring a property.

The best case scenario is to hope that the initial test does not find any asbestos in your property. However, even with that, you might be better off buying a property that was built in the 1990s or later just to be safe. The risk of asbestos is extreme and dangerous.

Mold

Mold is a serious threat that can develop in any property, but it is common in damp areas. Mold builds up when an area is too wet or humid. Homes or other properties that have been subjected to flooding or extreme weather conditions are more likely to develop mold than others. Sometimes a property that is not maintained or cleaned properly could develop this problem.

Mold can be extremely dangerous. It can cause allergic reactions and breathing difficulties in anyone. Mold spores can get into your body and damage your lungs. Mold spores are also small enough that they could spread well beyond where they originate; it only takes a few gusts of wind or air moving for mold to travel around the entire property.

The Inspection Process

Mold in a home can be identified by a series of fungal growths that might be dark in color. Sometimes a strange, musty smell can be identified in areas where mold is growing.

Several steps are used for identifying mold:

1. The areas that an inspector must inspect include bathrooms, drywall surfaces, an attic, a basement, or any other space where water might be found. Outside patios and wood materials should also be inspected.

2. The impacted area needs to be treated with a humidifier.

Like with asbestos, it is easy for mold spores to spread when the air is dry. A bit of moisture in the air keeps the spores from dispersing.

3. A cleaner will have to be used on any surfaces that contained mold. These include any tiles, under carpets, any wall surfaces, or even some wood areas, like baseboards.

Sometimes an entire surface will have to be replaced if there is too much mold.

4. A mixture of bleach and water should be applied to the area that needs to be cleaned.

5. Any debris leftover must be vacuumed away.

6. Old surfaces that were removed can now be replaced.

7. The area needs to be tested one last time to ensure that the mold has been removed.

The mold removal process is critical to keeping your investment protected. It can cost $500 to $1,000 to have a property tested for mold. It may cost twice as much to get it removed and retested.

Lead Paint

Lead paint is one material that has been used that many owners might not let you know about. Some people will not tell you that a property contains lead paint because they are afraid the resale value will go decrease. Lead paint is dangerous and harmful. It will most likely be found on painted surfaces of a property that is older in age.

Lead paint was used in many properties to keep the paint strong and durable. Lead could also resist moisture and make it easier for the paint to dry.

Lead paint can be dangerous to anyone who comes in contact with it, especially children. Dust from lead paint and exposure to any particles that fall or chip off of a lead-painted area and if they are ingested can cause lead poisoning. This results in nervous system and kidney damage. It can also cause stunted or delayed growth in children. Lead materials have a sweet taste to them, thus making them attractive to children who do not know better.

Is Lead Still Used?

Today lead paint has been outlawed in many countries around the world. It was outlawed in the United States in 1977. It was also banned in the United Kingdom. Various laws about how lead paint may be used are also in place in Canada, Australia, New Zealand, Brazil, China, and many other countries.

However, there are some countries where investment properties might still have lead paint. Japan, India, Malaysia, Peru, and much of Africa do not have any laws that restrict lead paint usage. A 2015 Toxics Link study found that nearly a third of all properties in India use lead paint. Algeria and South Africa are the only two countries in Africa that have specific laws restricting how lead paint can be used.

Age Is a Factor

Check on the age of any property you want to invest in. Any property that was built before 1980 should be inspected to see if it contains any lead paint. An Environmental Protection Agency report says that around 25 percent of properties in the United States built from 1960 to 1977 contain lead paint. That number increases to 69 percent for homes built from 1940 to 1959. As well, 87 percent of properties built before 1940 are likely to contain lead paint.

The worst part is that some of those older homes might have lead paint hiding underneath newer layers of paint. Although a newer layer of paint might shield people from the lead, there is still a potential for the lead surface to chip or crack. This, in turn, causes lead particles to come loose and become dangerous. Therefore, any older property must be tested for lead regardless of how intense and thorough the new paint job might be.

How Lead Is Found and Removed

Although you could paint over a layer of lead paint, it is best that you get that layer removed altogether. Sometimes the chipping of the under layer can hamper the addition of new layers.

The process for finding and removing old lead paint in a property is critical for ensuring the property is safe to be in.

1. Small bits of paint can be chipped off a surface and sent to a professional lab for testing.

2. Lift up corners of carpet and have a sample of the painted area underneath tested. The paint has to be wet so it will not spread around.

3. A chemical stripper or scraping device has to be applied to any surface that contains lead paint.

4. A vacuum must be used to remove all the lead paint bits that were removed.

5. After the lead is completely removed, a new coating of paint can be used on the surface. Some additional epoxy materials or crack filler may also be required if the surface has cracks and joins showing.

It will cost around $300 to $400 to have your property tested for lead paint. The removal process can cost at least $800 although that total will be higher if you have more areas that need to be treated.

Lead Pipes

The water pipes within a property should be checked. Have a full inspection of the plumbing system in a property to see if there are lead pipes. Lead pipes had been used in many homes up until the mid-1980s. Lead particles can come off some older pipes and get into a property's water supply. All old lead pipes have to be removed and replaced as soon as possible.

A plumbing team can inspect the pipes using a camera. If the pipes are found to have lead, a digging project may be required to remove those pipes and replace them with new ones. This could cost $1,000 or more.

The risk of lead, mold and other harmful materials can be significant in some older investment properties. It is your responsibility to recognize and correct any problems once you have purchased the property. Many times the inspection prior to purchase will highlight these problems.

The potential for you to manage negotiations and to move them forward might be easy if you incorporate the costs of removing the problems identified within a property. Prior to making an offer, be sure you consider what you will need to do to adjust the value of a property if any hazards are found or if you can persuade the seller to cover the costs associated with certain problems.

Chapter 18: Structural Issues In a Property

While mold, asbestos, and other hazardous materials can be a threat in your home, you have to consider the actual construction of the building you are contemplating purchasing. Is it structurally sound and secure?

Many older investment properties might have suffered from a lot of damage and wear and tear over time. In many instances, a property could have been impacted by significant weather issues or natural disasters. These include floods and earthquakes for the most part. The natural shifting of soil can also cause problems in some properties.

Structural issues might make it harder for you to get the financing needed for the property. A building would have to be fixed and reinforced to ensure it is safe. You won't be able to get the financing you want if those problems exist.

What Problems Can Develop?

There are many problems that can occur within a property. An inspector will list all the problems he finds with the property and help you understand what needs to be done in any situation.

Foundation

The foundation must be inspected carefully. All visible or accessible parts of your foundation have to be inspected. These include the floor or slab, and walls of the foundation. A concrete slab at the bottom may damaged by tree roots. Are there any cracks in surfaces and has the foundation moved? Cracks or wear in the foundation might be a sign that the stability of the house is in jeopardy. It could cause the frame to weaken.

Basement or Crawl Space

Many residential investments, particularly older ones, have basements or crawl spaces under the house. These are great areas for storage or recreational uses, but there are often drainage problems or water seepage. Excess moisture and humidity can develop in some situations. While a water pump or other device that can remove water from an area can be used for water problems, there are often risks associated when such a pump stops working.

Frame

The framing of a home has to adhere to certain building standards and codes which are set by the municipality or state. An inspection is required at framing stage and every stage of building. The frame is often made of wood and includes various water and weather barriers and insulation features to keep the building intact, dry, and sturdy. Other materials in the construction process will cover up the frame, such as the outside sheeting and inside drywall.

Sometimes scanning units may help with finding places where wood inside a building has deteriorated. Heat signatures can also be used to find insects in an area. This is especially vital for finding termites and dry rot.

Roof

The roof should be checked to see that it is a solid and sturdy cover for the home. While the tiles on the top of the roof are important, the sheathing used to create the roof over the rafters should also be inspected to see that it is sturdy and has not deteriorated.

Any leaks in a roof should be checked. While they can be patched up easily, it is even more important to see what caused the leaks to develop. The same sensors used on the frame can be used for the roof to identify any problems or weak areas.

The gutters around the roof can be inspected. The gutters will have to be aligned properly so they can redirect water away from the property. This keeps precipitation from seeping into the ground and impacting the foundation. Poorly operating gutters can make it harder for a property to stay dry.

Flooring Surfaces

You can tell there are problems with the floor when the surface is warped or uneven. Creaking sounds can be a sign of real trouble. Those sounds can be a sign that the joints and supports under the home are worn. The supports could also be weak and make the floor give in spots.

Individual joints and surfaces might have to be replaced and repaired. Sometimes the surface underneath the floor will have to be opened up to get these parts reattached or strengthened. The general goal is to keep the surface sturdy and less likely to wear out. Sometimes the carpet or tiles on the floor might have to be replaced, but that is generally cosmetic.

How to Resolve the Issues

The following steps should help you identify issues that need attention:

1. Contact an appropriate inspector to reviewing the property.

An inspector will identify all the problems that might be found in the home.

2. The inspector should come out to the property with the appropriate instruments to identify problems relating to wood damage, termites, mold, dry rot, and so forth.

The inspector should be able to review moisture areas, heat signatures, and other issues in a home without the need to cut through any surface.

3. Any problems that were identified should be discussed between you and the inspector.

4. Depending on the recommendations, you will have to get a proper contractor out to a property to get the issues attended to.

The contractor you hire should be one experienced with roofs, frames, or foundation repairs. Make sure you review the professional's services before choosing to work with someone in particular. This is to ensure you have the right person to help you with suggestions for resolving any issues.

5. You might have to get multiple contractors dedicated to very specific parts of your property.

Arrangements for different contractors in the correct order will have to be made and timing will be critical so that you can have use of your property as soon as possible.

What Will it Cost?

Even though the structural problems in a property are not of your doing, you will still have to spend money to get these problems fixed up as soon as possible. You would have to incorporate some of these expenses into the cost associated with acquiring the property. This is particularly for cases where the homeowner that you are getting a property off of might not have the money to pay for any repairs on one's own.

The cost to repair the structure issues can vary based on intensity. You might have to spend $500 to $2,000 on most repairs. You could spend $10,000 or more if you need to get an entire foundation replaced.

The worst part is that some issues might be significant enough to where you would have to tear down an entire property. This comes as the existing property could be too unsafe due to significant structural issues that might be found.

These points make it all the more important for you to watch for how you negotiate your deal with a home seller. You can talk about the new things that a property requires and what it might cost to get such repairs handled. This could help you get a sale of a property for a little cheaper.

Be aware of the issues that come with structural damages when finding a property you want to invest in. Such damages can be significant and may keep a property from being worth as much as you want it to be. Getting those damages fixed up and resolved soon can make a difference for keeping the value of the property reasonable.

Chapter 19: Planning a Purse Offer

After you find a real estate investment that you want, you can prepare a purse offer. This refers to the general amount of money you are willing to pay for the property for sale. This is a vital part of the investment process as it directly determines what you will actually spend on the property.

All the points you have read about so far relate to finding a good property and determining the factors that might influence its value and how to get them resolved. After you decide what you want to invest in the property after determining its appropriate value, you can make the appropriate purse offer. You should have more than enough information on the property at this point.

The greatest concern about a purse offer is that it needs to be not only a sensible offer but also include several vital conditions. Having sensible terms and conditions ensures you will have an easier time with negotiating and buying the property at an acceptable price for both you and the seller.

Base Your Offer on the Right Factors

You must decide on a proper offer based on many critical factors so the total value of your offer is appropriate and suitable.

The Original Valuation

As you read earlier in this guide, you will need to have the property evaluated. This is to get a clear idea of what a property might be worth. You have to know this so you have a base guideline for what you will offer the owner/seller of the property.

You certainly don't have to stay with the exact value of the appraisal. You might want to offer slightly more than the appraised value so that the owner would be encouraged to sell the property.

What Can You Afford?

Decide what you can actually afford when making an offer. You will have already spoken with a lender/banker and looked over your financial situation. You now know the amount of loan you qualify for, what the terms of the loan will be, and the monthly payments. You have also estimated the cost of utilities and any repairs or renovations that will be needed should you succeed in purchasing the property.

You have the option to pay cash for the property. This will depend on the amount of cash you have at your disposal and the amount of cash you will have to hold back for evaluation and inspection reports, repairs, renovations, and legal fees. In fact, there is a chapter later in this guide that covers whether you should use cash or financing.

You must look into various points relating to your property based on what you know you can handle. These include such points as:

- The total value of the property based on the evaluation.

- How much you qualify for should you require a mortgage.

- Any inspections, repairs, or renovations that you need to make on the property.

- The interest rate of the loan; calculate interest you would pay over the time of the loan.

- The closing cost; you might have to spend about 5 percent of the property's value on the closing cost associated with a loan.

- Commissions will not be your worry as they are paid to the realtor by the seller from the proceeds of the sale.

The Proper Down Payment

The greater the down payment you have on hand for the purchase, the smaller the loan will have to be. What is more important is that a good down payment is needed to have your offer considered. If you can produce an offer that features a 20 percent down payment, this shows that you are serious and are capable of affording the property

You can always produce an offer with a larger down payment. You could offer a 30 or 40 percent down payment if you wish. A seller might be more interested at this point because you showing how committed you are to the property. Having a larger down payment makes the mortgage smaller and you could possibly arrange for a shorter term for the mortgage which decreases the interest to be paid over the life of the loan.

What Is the Seller's Price?

You have to look at the seller's price when deciding on your offer. Although the overall evaluation process and your personal plans are important, you cannot ignore what the seller wants. A seller might use one of many strategies to determine the price of the property:

1. A seller could have used someone else for the evaluation process. This is best as it ensures a fair process is used for determining the value.

2. A seller might also overprice the house. This allows for some room for negotiating.

3. Other sellers might price their properties too high. The seller might be focused on that price and does not want to negotiate.

4. People might even offer their properties at a value well below its actual value. A seller could do this to get many buyers out to a property. This starts a bidding war that could become profitable to the seller.

The Prices of Other Properties In An Area

You have to look at the prices of other properties in the area. These prices can vary and could be high depending on the area.

The most important point here is to look at prices of properties similar to yours. This is to create a good base for how you will determine the amount of your offer. You have to work with properties similar to yours based on:

- Layout

- Size

- Functionality

- The age of the property

- Architectural design

- It's location to certain amenities

Check on any property similar to the one you want to buy and determine a value that is comparable to other properties in the area.

Review the Market

Consider the economic market. This goes beyond just the values of properties in an area. How is the market changing? Are the prices of properties going up or down?

The value of a property is relative to how the market is moving. If the market is going up, you could expect a slightly higher value to the property. This could be reflective of what the property could be worth in a few months or years from now based on the growing market.

Every real estate market is different. Some markets might be very healthy while others could be weak. It is also impossible to predict how these markets might change over time.

Unique Features Relating to the Property

You could set a value for the property based on the unique features that it has. There might be certain qualities to a property that you feel could be extremely important. These include:

- The proximity of the property to a school or other amenities.

- A distinct architectural feature of the property.

- Any technical features that make a property outstanding, such as renewable energy features.

- Any historical points relating to the property.

You might want to offer a little more than what the home is worth if you can identify anything special about the property that makes it unique and a worthwhile investment. Offering something extra helps you to have a better chance of acquiring the property.

Additional Considerations

You have the option to add various conditions to your offer. Excessive conditions could discourage the seller to accept your offer. The conditions will be part of the negotiations with the seller.

Pass an Inspection

You can add the requirement for a property to pass an inspection before you buy it. As you read earlier, an inspection is required, not only for your safety and peace of mind, but also to fulfill the requirements of a lender.

You can always add conditions like any costs associated with repairing or inspecting a property would be covered by the seller. You could establish a limit to the value the seller would be willing to cover. Of course, the total repairs needed could influence the value of the property and that would be reflected in your offer.

Repairs Must Be Made

You could ask the seller to make all repairs before you draft a contract to complete the sale. You could offer a value slightly higher than the actual home's worth to help cover the costs associated with the repairs.

Be reasonable as you do not want the homeowner to refuse your offer because you were too demanding in affecting the repairs. You can use a cap on how much money you are willing to accept for the repairs.

Your Property Must Sell

Are you trying to sell a property you own while looking a new investment? You could add a stipulation to your offer stating that your property must sell before your offer goes forward. This adds a bit of assurance stating that you will not get into the transaction unless anything you have is sold off properly.

Your purse offer can also include a term where the old investment must sell before you can accept the purchase of the new property. You may want to use the old property to pay off the new one in lieu of a traditional loan.

A home seller will appreciate this because you will show you are committed to the sale by adding the stipulation that you will complete the purchase pending the sale of your other property.

Qualify For a Loan

You can always use a loan or other form of financing if you do not have a property you wish to sell. It could be easy for you to get a good loan on your property investment. It is even easier for you to get a loan if you have a great credit rating. No matter what happens, you have to actually qualify for a loan before you can buy a property unless you are paying cash. Almost all realtors will insist that you pre-qualify for a mortgage before making an offer on any property.

Qualifying for a loan is easy if you have a good credit rating. A greater down payment could also help as it decreases the amount of a mortgage. You could get a lower interest rate on your loan when a larger down payment is offered.

You have to establish a smart offer that is realistic and appealing to the seller. This is all about giving you a better chance of getting the property you want.

Chapter 20: Monthly Payments

Unless you are paying cash for a property, you will have to make monthly payments to a lender/bank. You will need to make appropriate payments on your property based its value, the type of financing, and any other charges that might arise.

Expect the costs will go beyond the initial cost associated with buying the property and any other charges that might come with the purchase process. Regular monthly charges are important to see as they can add to the total cost of owning a property. In fact, you will have to spend money on all of these expenses even if you do not plan on actually living in the property that you have purchased.

Note: Although parts of this chapter are not applicable to people who paid cash for a property without the need of any loans or financing, some of the monthly expenses will still apply.

Interest Charges

A loan or financing plan will clearly have interest charges. You can aim to reduce the interest charges based on your credit rating and your down payment. For instance, you might get a property that costs $185,000 while making a 20% down payment of $37,000 on the property. That would leave you with $148,000 that you owe on the property.

You could arrange for a 30-year fixed rate mortgage loan at 5.19%. You would have to spend $812 per month on the principal and interest. If the rate was reduced to 4.29%, you would spend $732 per month on the loan.

If you had made a 30% down payment of $55,500 on the property, this could cut the monthly principal and interest charge down to $640 at a 4.29% interest rate.

Property Tax

You will have to pay property taxes on your investment. The tax will vary based on the area. As you read earlier, the property taxes on your property could be very high. They could also be nonexistent in some parts of the world.

Property taxes are payable whether or not you have a mortgage. These taxes are collected by the government or municipality where the property is located.

Other Fees

Various additional fees will be part of your monthly payments. The greatest concern for these fees is that they are points that might be incorporated into the property expenses regardless of what you are investing in. You will not have any control over these fees either; they cannot be included in the contract for a property.

These include charges like:

- Home insurance costs.

- Homeowner's association fees.

- Regular utility costs.

- Municipal services; these include services for managing garbage pick-up, road maintenance.

Check with reports on any market you want to invest in to see what the fees might be.

You will have to pay these charges regardless of whether you live in the property you are investing in or not.

Chapter 21: Dealing With Multiple Offers

The real estate investment field has become a multi-billion dollar industry the world over. There is always an immense amount of competition when trying to make a deal on a property.

Sometimes an investment property could be so popular that several people will make offers to acquire it. A property could be located in a profitable or viable area. It might be in an area where more rent can be charged or there are a number of long-term tenants.

What's more is that the competition you might encounter for a single property could be rather tough. You might find some competition that has a better chance of purchasing the property you are interested in by being able to offer better offers. This includes people who might have more money than you or access to a better financing plan. Others might include a group where everyone pools their resources to acquire a property.

Make Many Bids If Possible

You can always make multiple bids on a property. These bids can be made based on the number of people who are trying to invest in the same property. You might need to make multiple offers in the event a property is being bid on by many people.

One bid might be listed with a larger down payment but with a smaller total cost of selling price of the property. Another bid could include a few terms for having repairs done. You have the option to do anything you want with your offer. You only need to present your offer to the seller and wait for a reply. If the seller states they have a better offer, you most likely will be given the opportunity to make another offer. However, you will not be told what the other offers were. You have to make a judgment call as to what your new offer will be. Having an offer that is unique and stipulates different features, requests, and concessions will help.

Look for Multiple Properties

You could also look for many properties in a local area. It might be difficult to secure a property if there are lots of people bidding on it. Fortunately, you can improve your chances by bidding on multiple properties. You can search for similar properties in a local region and be prepared to make offers on each. This could increase your chances of getting into a certain market while also diversifying the types of properties you are bidding on.

You can even place bids on multiple properties held by the same person in the region. This gives that person the impression that you are committed to finding a property in that area. Remember, you do not have to actually buy a property if the seller agrees to work with your bid; it is your choice as to which agreements you want to make.

The values of the bids you make should vary with each property. That is, you cannot just assume that one strategy should work for every single property. The number of competitors for each property will vary as well.

Can You See What Others Are Offering?

Naturally, you might feel a desire to want to know what other people are offering for the same property you are attempting to purchase. You might want to know the other offers so that you can adjust your offer to make it more acceptable to the seller.

The problem is that offers are sealed. These offers are kept private to ensure that people do not try to get a leg up in the bidding process.

You can always get information online about recent sales in the area. You can look at the bids for those sales to see how they varied and what made certain bids accepted. A title search or research into a property realtor's records might help you determine what people have tried offering for certain properties.

There is always a chance that you might have a better bid at the outset.

Chapter 22: Getting Sellers to Compete For You

The competition is not always you competing with other prospective buyers. You could encourage other sellers to compete for your business. That is, they will notice that you are in the market and will try to entice you to buy a property with one of the various offers. They will want to get you on board as a buyer.

Those sellers will notice that you are interested in and could be a viable investor. In most cases, a seller will want to get in touch with you not because you have money but rather because a seller just wants to sell his property. That seller may be trying to take advantage of the market or just to sell the property before it becomes too difficult for someone to afford. You might be surprised that sellers will want to get in touch with you as a prospective buyer.

Use Fewer Contingencies

One idea to make you attractive to home sellers is to use fewer contingencies. Sellers will appreciate you more when you are willing to buy a property as-is. No one likes to contend with lots of hang-ups and red tape. Using fewer contingencies shows that you are not demanding and that you are willing to buy the property no matter the condition.

Keep Your Finances in Check

Always make sure your finances are in order when trying to find a property. Show that you have financing ready or that you have enough cash on hand. This might require providing information of your income to sellers or any lines of credit you will use. Having more information helps you demonstrate that you are committed to the transaction.

Respond Quickly

Let the sellers who contact you know right away what your response is. This will let the seller know that you are really interested. Remember, you are not obligated to go forward with your offer. You could increase your offer or walk away from the property. You will lose only the money that accompanied your offer, which may have been $1000 or $2000. At the point of your offer, you have not committed money for the down payment. The down payment is paid and the mortgage is finalized when the offer is accepted and the contract has been made for the purchase.

What About Counter Offers?

There might be times when counter offers might be possible. A counter offer would be a response to the original offer you have made. You can always wait a few days to respond with a counter offer.

The seller might be soliciting counter offers from other people. If you know there has been multiple offers on a property (your real estate agent will give you this information), it might be to your advantage to make a counter offer quickly.

Chapter 23: Cash or Financing?

As you get ready to acquire a property, you will have to decide how you will pay for it. You have one of two options to work with when buying a property:

1. You can choose to pay for the property in cash.

2. You can also arrange for financing to paying for the property over a long-term.

Cash

A cash payment is self-explanatory. This is all about getting a property paid off through a straightforward one-time payment.

Many people are able to buy homes for cash and they avoid many of the expenses that come with financing. A straight cash transaction does not entail any interest charges, mortgage fees, or other dues.

Sellers love it when people buy properties with cash. The risk of the buyer pulling out due to a lack of funding is eliminated.

The home is not leveraged when it is paid for with cash either. That is, the buyer is not using borrowed money. Therefore, he can sell the property quickly. That person does not have to cover the full cost of a loan after a sale takes place. The owner can sell the property quickly regardless of the market conditions. That owner could even sell it at a loss if it becomes necessary.

How Would the Cash Be Delivered?

The cash payment must be delivered carefully and safely.

You would have to deliver the cash to the other party by one of three options:

1. A certified check could be sent out to the seller. This should come from a checking account. That money could have been acquired through a loan that you moved into that account.

2. A wire transfer can be utilized to get money from one bank account to the account that the seller holds. Fees might be charged for a wire transfer, although those charges would vary.

3. Online wallet transactions can also be utilized. This is provided that you and the other party both have the same online wallet program.

4. Money can be held in escrow with your lawyer and he can make sure the legal documents are completed and the money transferred to the owner to complete the sale.

The problem with using physical cash is that the money could be seen as suspicious. The government might also become suspicious and start looking into all your financial affairs and transactions to see if there might be illegal money laundering involved. There is also the risk that all that physical cash could be lost or stolen while in transit.

The other options are safer and ensure that the money moves through smoothly and carefully. It does take a few business days for the money to move along depending on the transaction you complete.

Offering Proof

You must offer proof that you have the cash on hand to make a transaction. You could always share information on your online wallet or checking accounts. You obviously would not share the specifics of any account that you have until the actual transaction takes place. By offering some kind of proof, you are at least letting the other party know that you are serious about making the deal.

Outright Ownership

A vital aspect of getting your property paid off completely entails how you will hold ownership over your property. Since you will not owe anything to the original seller, you will have full control over your property. You will not be subjected to any restrictions by that seller.

When you use financing, you would have to work with a series of rules and regulations for what you can and cannot do with the property. The lender might not approve of plans your have for renovating a property. Lenders would still allow you to rent out your property and provide you with income, but some might be stringent as to whom you could and could not be allowed on your property. Paying for a property with cash keeps you from being subjected to such rules.

Get a Leg Up on Negotiations

A huge part of paying for a property with cash is that negotiations will be easy. Property sellers are often more likely to accept offers from buyers who are ready to pay cash for the property.

Bidding wars can be a challenge. A seller will immediately consider your offer if it is cash to buy the property. Your chances of winning a bidding war will be significantly higher with cash than it would be otherwise.

Can This Work Through a Loan?

People often get the cash they need for direct payments for property through banking accounts or wire transfers. Sometimes the money can come directly from the sale of a property that a person might have sold to get the funds needed for acquiring the new property. Not all people will have access to the money needed to pay cash for the total asking price. This is where a loan can come in handy.

You can always use a loan to cover a direct cash payment. A loan could be provided to you through an outside bank or credit union. The loan can be given to you with unique terms that might be simplified. This is convenient, but you will have to investigate the terms of a loan. You must analyze what the loan expenses and rates are and what the overall cost for your property might be.

You would have to compare what a bank loan might offer versus what a property sales agent might provide you through a financing deal. Sometimes the bank loan might cost more than a financing plan.

Financing Through the Seller

There might be times where you will not get enough money on hand to pay for the entire property value. This might be due to many factors including not being able to secure a loan large enough to cover the entire cost of the property. You can still buy the real estate you wish to invest in through a financing plan.

A seller can help you with establishing a financing plan. This is often done through the support of a bank or other lending group that the seller is associated with. You can use this in the event you do not have all the money needed, and you have been unable to get it from a lender that is not affiliated with the seller.

Financing is best if you plan on getting the money you need for the property and make regular payments on the property. This is convenient as it gives you a little more freedom for funding an investment. You can also get this to work if you have a regular income to work with. The money you earn from your employment or other investments you have could help you to cover the costs associated with the financing.

Financing is also great for when you need to get lots of repairs on a property. You can use a financing plan to cover not only the cost of the home but also the estimated expenses relating to repairing it.

Many expenses could be added to the total value of the property. You would have to review the financing that a seller is willing to offer and see how well it might work in your favor.

Down Payment

The down payment, as you read earlier, refers to the payment you must make to secure the loan. The payment is often 20 percent or more of the loan. The remaining 80 percent will be subjected to interest charges and monthly payments that you would make.

Some financing providers might provide you with the option to make in a larger down payment to obtain a lower interest rate if you have the cash to increase the down payment.

Interest Rate

The interest rate is an expense that is used to support the financing process. A lender needs to cover the cost associated with maintaining the loan and ensuring the bank can continue to offer its services.

The interest rate can vary based on the condition of the market and the down payment you made on the property. This rate might be as little as 3 percent or even up to 6 percent. Sometimes your credit rating might influence the rate, thus causing you to spend more on interest if you have a poor rating.

The rate might be fixed during the entire life of the loan. Considering how most financing plans for homes are for thirty years, this might be a difficult problem. Fortunately, some lenders offer adjustable rates that change in accordance with the market. You might also refinance your loan to get a more favorable rate provided the market rate has declined.

Origination Fee

An origination fee is charged by many lenders to process the loan. The fee is used to cover the application for the loan, arranging for the funds and figuring out the overall payment plan for the loan. This fee should be about 1 percent of the total cost of the home. You might be able to negotiate a lower origination fee on the loan if the property value is very high.

Closing Costs

Although it sounds like something you would put at the end, the closing costs is also charged at the start of the loan term. This is technically to close the deal, arrange for payments to the seller, and set up the payment plan for the buyer.

There are many things that go into the closing costs. These often include:

- Appraisal fees for determining the value of the property.

- Title search charges.

- Added costs for registering and filing the title for the property.

- Charges for any land surveys.

- Any title or homeowners insurance policies that have to be established.

- Discount points; these refer to fees that may be spent to lower the total interest on the loan.

Are There Restrictions?

While you would have full control of a property if you pay for it in cash, this might not be the case when you acquire an investment property through a financing plan. Your financing provider might keep you from being able to adjust or change your property.

A finance provider might allow you to repair the property but might prevent you from making any other modifications to the property. You might not be allowed to renovate a property or change the floor plan. You could be restricted from adding any new additions or detached buildings to your property.

This does not mean that the financing partner will not allow to do anything with your property. You can always get in touch with the financing provider to ask about something you want to do with your property. This is provided you have enough details on what you want to do. You could explain to the financier about your intentions, how you will plan it, and what benefit it will offer. The financier might approve of your proposal if there is a clear benefit that would cause the property's value to increase, but there are no guarantees that the lender would actually agree.

Common Expenses for Both Choices

Although cash and financing are both different, you should be aware of a few expenses that you will have to spend for either setup.

Escrow

The first common expense is the escrow charge. The escrow refers to a total amount of money that you will spend on your home and have held by a third-party. It is a deposit of money that will be delivered to the seller after the transaction has been completed.

The escrow ensures that a transaction will move forward as planned. The third-party responsible for holding the escrow payment will not transfer the money until both sides have completed the agreement.

Once the transaction is finalized, and both sides have agreed and signed off, the money from the escrow account will be transferred. The seller will get the money from the buyer.

The escrow charge might be added to a financing plan. This could be about 0.5 to 1 percent of the value of the property during the life of the loan. The escrow charge is applied to ensure that both sides are satisfied legally. For a straightforward cash payment, the 0.5 to 1 percent value will be charged by the escrow holder all at once.

You and the other party in the transaction will be responsible for determining who will pay for the escrow. An individual bank or other financial service providers may be contacted to act as the escrow. There should be no referral fees involved with whoever the escrow holder might be.

Taxes and Insurance

Taxes and insurance charges may also be added to a property. These could total around 1 to 2 percent of the home's value during the overall transaction.

Taxes can vary based on where the property is. These include both property and sales taxes alike. Income taxes might also be charged depending on how you use the property. Check with the laws where you are to identify all the applicable taxes.

Loan insurance charges are also needed to ensure that the seller can be paid in the event any issues come about with regards to your efforts to pay off the property. Loan insurance totals applied by the lender/bank.

Use Cash If...

Now that you understand how the two options work, you should think about when they are appropriate. You can use cash to pay for a home if:

- You wish to get full control of the property.

- You have plans for renovating a property.

- You do not plan on having that property for a long time.

- You do not have regular access to your property.

- There is enough money either by the cash you have or through an outside loan to cover the cost of the home.

Use Financing If...

Do not forget about the financing option when paying for a property. You can use the financing to cover the cost of your property if:

- You plan on holding a property for an extended period of time.

- The property needs to be repaired.

- You do not have any need to modify your property in any way after it has been fully repaired.

- You plan to live or work in your property or will be close enough to check in on it regularly.

- You need assistance through a seller's financing provider to purchase the property.

- There are funds available to cover all the expenses relating to a financing plan.

- You are aiming to use the property to raise income through rent or tenants.

Chapter 24: The Auction Process

Have you ever been on one of those online auction sites? You might have found some intriguing deals on everyday products through one of those sites. Maybe you found something for sale at an auction that you might not have been able to find elsewhere. eBay and other similar auction sites have truly impacted the retail world and have changed the way people make purchases.

Maybe you have seen physical auctions where people bid on items that they want to acquire. These auctions often have high-value products like vehicles seized by lenders or other authorities or collectible items of high-value. The thrill of watching an auction can be intriguing as you hear someone calling out numbers and names while many people try to buy something at a certain price.

Today you can find real estate investments on the auction block and online. You can place your own bid. There is a potential for you to get a great deal on a property through an auction, but there is also a risk that you might spend more than you can afford.

The Basic Concept of the Auction

Have you participated in an online auction before? If so, then you know how an auction works. It is all about having the highest bid. You would compete with many others who are interested in the same property.

The auction is designed to help people find properties that might be cheaper than what is in the market. The potential for the value of a property to change during the auction process is something you cannot ignore.

What Will You Find at an Auction?

The properties you will find at a real estate auction are all worth investigating. You should understand why they are on the auction block to begin with. These are all properties that were owned by people at some point in the past and have lost the rights to continue to own them.

The most common type of property you will find on the auction block is a foreclosed property. You have read about how foreclosed properties work earlier in this guide. When a property is in foreclosure, the bank that was owed the money will offer the property to the public to try to sell it. The bank will want to get it sold and off of the market soon so the losses that entity has incurred will not be too great.

Some auction properties are ones that were seized by the government. These include properties that were held by people who have been sent to prison. These properties would be on the auction block because the lender needs to a way to get back the money lost in the investment.

How Many People Can Participate in an Auction?

There are no real rules as to how many people can participate in a certain auction. You might find auctions where you are competing with one or two other people. Sometimes the party responsible for hosting the auction might have limits to how many people can participate at a given time. These rules are designed to ensure that only those who can actually pay for a home can participate. This would entail pre-registration.

How to Participate in An Auction

There are several steps that can be used help you participate in a home auction. Be advised that the process entails more than just showing up to a particular event.

1. Visit an auction to see what happens.

The best way to understand how a real estate auction works is to attend one. Learn about how people bid on properties. Getting a first-hand look at how an auction works can help you understand what happens in the process and how you could save money on purchasing a property.

2. Check on when the auction will take place.

An auction house will provide information on when and where a home auction will occur. Many auction providers will let people know about when the auction will take place at least a month ahead of time. Some might advertise an even earlier notice to attract more prospective bidders. This advance notice gives people enough time to see what properties are available and to also arrange for the money needed.

3. Review the properties that will be made available in the auction.

An auction house must have information on the properties that will be included in the actual auction. A listing of lots should be disclosed. The listing should include detailed information on every property being offered.

The auction house must be as direct and open about the property as possible. A listing should include details on:

- Where the property is located.

- What the property features.

- The reason why the property is on the auction block.

- The value of the property or a minimum bid; this is the first value that the property will be available for during the auction itself.

You must research the properties available for sale before the auction takes place.

Visit the physical location of a property if you can. You could get a good idea of what that building is like so you know if it is the right one to bid on. Whatever you do, avoid disturbing any occupants inside the home. Do not trespass on the property either. It is illegal to trespass on a property or bother someone inside the house; it could result in criminal action against you.

Some auction houses might offer open houses where bidders can view inside the house before the auction. This helps to not only increase the prospective number of bidders but to possibly increase the potential bid values. Not all providers will offer open houses. See what an auction house will provide you when looking at a possible open house event.

Consider the potential repairs or renovations that a property might need and the costs. Some of the homes on the auction block may be in disrepair. These include homes that were owned by criminals who might have neglected their properties or people who could not afford those homes and left them in bad shape.

Of course, a property that is in disrepair will surely have a lower value. It might be available with a lower opening bid because of that. You would still have to factor in the repair costs to go alongside your main bid. The repairs will be your responsibility if your bid is accepted. Your bid will buy the home as-is.

4. Get pre-approved for a loan or prepare enough cash for the auction.

People who wish to participate in home auctions will have to show they have the money to take part in the event. Auction houses are not going to just let anyone into the event. An auction house will need proof from all prospective bidders that they have the money needed to actually acquire a property.

A typical auction house will accept cash, a check, or a money order. You will have to pay the entire value of the property immediately after the auction if you win it. You must provide the appropriate funds right away regardless of whether you have a cash payment right now or if you have a loan that can be used as payment.

5. Check on the pre-auction deposit.

A deposit should be placed on a property of interest before you bid on it. All bidders must put in their pre-auction deposits beforehand so they can qualify to participate in the auction. Auction houses require these deposits to ensure that the people bidding on the property are sincere.

The pre-auction deposit is typically 5 to 10 percent of the value of what the final bid is expected to be. The auction house will determine that approximate final bid value. This is no guarantee that the final bid will be what the auction house says it will be; the actual bid could be higher or lower. All parties that did not win the auction will have their deposits returned to them. The only money the auction house will hold on to is the money from the bidder who actually won the auction.

This is the registration you must follow to get into the auction. You have to have the deposit to ensure you will participate in the auction.

6. Confirm the details of the auction beforehand.

Sometimes an auction might be delayed or canceled. There are many reasons why this could happen:

- The auction could be canceled because the borrower of the property in question was able to come up with the money needed to avoid a foreclosure.

- The owner might have sold off the property to someone else in a short sale, thus taking it off the auction market.

- The owner could have successfully arranged a loan modification to make it easier for that person to pay off the property. This will also remove the property from the auction.

- An auction might be delayed because a bank or lender could not get enough documentation in time. The auction would be delayed allow the lender to have time to present the paperwork..

- An owner might also request more time to complete a short sale. The auction will be delayed at this point until further notice; the event will be back on if the owner cannot complete the sale and the property will be foreclosed upon.

Always confirm with the auction provider about the event. Do this even on the actual day of the auction if you have to. You must confirm all the details surrounding the auction beforehand.

7. Get to the auction and place your bids.

Get to the auction at least an hour before it starts. A bidding card should be available for you if you made your reservation and deposit. Reserve your seat and raise your bidding card when the auctioneer announces the price that you are willing to pay for the property. The length of the auction can vary based on how many people are participating in the event.

You could potentially win the property in the auction, but you must follow some additional steps if you do win. Just because you won the auction does not mean that it is finished and that the property in question is definitely yours.

What If You Win?

There are a few things that must be done in the event you win the auction. Although these rules are important, there is still a potential that the original owner of the property could have the property returned, thus keeping you from actually buying it:

1. After you win, you will have to present the money for the property to the auction operator.

You must present the money to the auction house immediately after you have won. You might also be allowed to present it the next business day. The terms will vary.

2. Complete a certificate of sale.

The certificate of sale is the document stating that you have acquired the property through the auction sale. This includes a certificate for the property and deed and any relevant tax forms relating to the property. The specifics of the certificate of sale and anything else that comes with it will vary by state or region.

3. Wait for your certificate of title.

It will take up to 10 days for you to receive the official certificate of title for your property. The certificate of title will state that you are the official owner of the property.

The original owner of the property could still get the property back up to this point. That owner might object to your purchase. That person could pay the total amount one owed in full to get the rights back to the property. In other words, you should not do anything with the property until you have actually received the certificate of title. Once you receive the official certificate of title, the original owner will no longer have access or control over the property. You will have full control over it at this point.

You will be reimbursed in full in the event the original owner does get the money to cover the debt that was owed. That is, the money you spent on the property will be sent back to you. Any loans or other forms of financing will be canceled; you should not have to spend anything on fees at this point, nor should your credit rating be impacted in any way. Think of this point as the last opportunity the original owner has to save his ownership status of the property.

Watch for Emotions

One thing you might notice while at a real estate auction is people engaging in certain actions to keep their feelings from being seen. People often try to keep their emotions in check during an auction. Sometimes clear emotional displays will give away what someone might be thinking when trying to acquire a property. This often causes other bidders to take action and to change their strategies for bidding.

The important thing to do when at a real estate auction is to avoid being caught up in your emotions. Stick with a strategy you have made with beforehand instead of bidding on something based on what you are feeling.

Displaying your emotions is more than just unprofessional. It also tips off other bidders about what you plan on doing. You will see many bidders doing numerous things to keep their emotions from showing:

- Many people wear sunglasses to keep their eyes from being visible.

- Stiff lips are often found on some people. They keep their lips shut, so they don't show a smile or frown.

- Many people might keep their hands in their pockets.

- Some bidders also wear hats to try and keep any facial muscles from being visible.

Sealed-Bid Auctions

One type of real estate auction is a sealed-bid auction. This is also referred to as a blind auction. All people bidding on the property will submit a sealed bid. These are prepared in advanced and given to the auction house at within a specific time. The main point is that each bidder will be unaware of whoever else is bidding on the property.

The person with the highest bid will buy the property. In other words, there are no ongoing actions where individuals can place multiple bids.

This is an interesting option for an auction as it reduces the emotional aspect of the process. It focuses more on people thinking about what they are willing to pay for a property. It requires an extensive amount of research into the property and a full understanding of what one would spend to cover costs relating to it. Plenty of thought would have to go into the final bid that someone wishes to submit.

Each participant should also think about how much to bid on a property in the event that a bid-off has to take place. This leads to the next important point.

What If There's a Tie?

There is always a chance at a sealed-bid auction could end in a tie. In this case, a bid-off would be set up. This would be done between the parties that tied for the highest bid at the start. Several steps will go into the process:

1. The parties that bid the most are called by the auction house.

The identification numbers of the bids may be called out. This ensures the names or identities of the people who placed those bids will not be revealed.

2. Each party will then write in a new value to bid.

The minimum bidding total should be whatever the original bid was. The auction house has the right to raise the total value of the minimum bid at this point. The house should also give each person a bid of extra time to figure out a new bid.

3. Every bid is then reviewed by the auction house. The party with the highest-value bid is the winner.

4. Another bid-off will take place between any other people who tie for the highest bid. This will go on until there is one certain party who absolutely bids more than anyone else.

The bid-off process is used to help get a sealed-bid auction running well enough. It keeps the process private and anonymous while also ensuring a fair system for running the event. Of course, those who get into a bid-off will surely notice just how much in demand a property might be as it gets to this point.

What About an Online Auction?

Online auctions have become rather popular. The growth of eBay is reflective of just how interested people are in online auctions. Today you can go online and find real estate for sale in many places around the online world.

An exciting part of real estate auctions is that they can be for properties from all corners of the world. Let's say you went to a site like Hubzu that offers online real estate auctions. You can search for properties in a specific geographic region. You can look for details on each property and take a virtual tour. You can then place a bid on the property if you are interested in it.

It is not hard to participate in an online auction provided you have a plan for doing so. The steps for entering into an online auction are as follows:

1. Find an appropriate website that lists real estate properties.

Sites like RealtyBid, Hubzu, Auction.com and many more are available for you to check out.

2. Check on any property you might be interested in.

While some properties are available for bidding now, others might be open in a few days. A site must include as much information as possible so you can get an idea of what is open.

You must do your own additional research on a property. You might ask for an official report on the value of the property or any historical points relating to it. Try and visit a property if it is located near you. Ask for information on the title, registration, and taxes.

3. Submit an appropriate payment to the auction.

You must register to use an auction site and then send in a deposit to the site. This refundable deposit should be worth a percentage of the minimum bid of the property you want to invest in. The money can be funded by a credit card that you register with the site. You will get the deposit back if you do not win the auction.

4. Get the financing arranged for the property in the event that you do win.

Get the appropriate financing information ready and present it to the auction site. This lists details on how you intend to pay for the property if you win. You can also present identity documents if you are bidding under a larger company name or trust.

5. Plan your bidding for the auction.

As the auction progresses, you will have the option to place a bid on a property. Check back regularly to see if the bid has increased. You might have to add a new bid if you still want the property.

A site might have the option for you to indicate a maximum bid. For instance, a minimum bid on a property might be for $50,000 with the value going up in increments of $5,000 at a time. You could state that your maximum bid would be $80,000.

Therefore, if you took the lead with a bid of $65,000, the total may stay the same. If someone bids $70,000, you will then have to increase your bid to $75,000 on the property. If another person bids $80,000, that person will be the leader.

You would have to manually submit another bid or change your maximum bid.

    6. Get in touch with the site if your bid won the auction.

You should review the purchase and sale agreement for the property if you have won. This should appear a few hours after the auction is over. You must review the timeframe for submitting all your documents for how you will pay for the property. You should have had these documents ready; submit them as soon as you can so the auction site will confirm the transaction.

You must submit everything the site asks for on time and as asked. You could risk not only losing the property but also your original deposit for entering the auction if you do not comply on time. After a while, you should get the title to the property. This will take a few business days the same as a traditional transaction.

Review the Buyer's Premium

Regardless of whether you get a property online or in person at an auction, you will have to pay a buyer's premium. This is a charge an auction house or website would charge to whoever wins the auction. The premium covers the cost associated with getting the property onto the auction block.

The average buyer's premium for a property is usually 5 percent of the winning bid. Factor this into the bidding process so you have a more realistic idea of what you will spend if you do win the auction.

Can You Really Save Money?

You might have gone online and read stories about people saving huge amounts of money on their real estate properties by getting them on the auction block. These include stories of people saying that they paid close to half of a property's actual value. These stories often give you the impression that you could save loads of money by getting a property at an auction.

Many properties are available for cheap prices thanks to the banks trying to unload them, but you are not always going to save money. The bidding process could be aggressive and competitive to the point where the cost of the property increases dramatically. You might also have to spend lots of money to restore and repair a property depending on its condition. You can never tell for sure how much money you will have to spend for the property.

You will have to devise a plan for bidding just like what you would for a regular home sale. Decide on the highest possible amount you are willing to spend on a property and don't waver. This should give you a bit of control over how you will bid.

Vital Terms to Watch For

Some terms should be reviewed for any auction you enter into. Any bids you wish to place must be made with all of these concerns in mind:

- Most auctions only accept cash purchases. That is, you cannot get financing on a property later. You have the option to secure a loan ahead of time to support a cash purchase.

- Any property you buy through an auction is sold as-is. You would be responsible for any repairs or other fixes that must be made on the property.

- The buyer's premium that is due before the auction will vary based on where the auction is being held. You must always cover this before entering the auction.

- The rules for submitting a bid will vary based on the auction. You might only be allowed to submit a bid if you can physically see the property or the auction site. Do not forget about registering for an auction.

An auction can make for a truly exciting and unique part of finding a real estate property to invest in. The possibilities surrounding the auction and the chances you have for saving big money on the property are worth looking into. Make sure you follow the rules of the auction and that you understand everything about the overall process.

Chapter 25: The Value of Title Insurance

Regardless of the property you plan on investing in, you have to get insurance on it to be fully protected against any occasion. Many insurance policies are available for various things relating to a property. These include fire and flood insurance policies and individual insurance plans that cover specific parts of a home. However, one type of insurance that you need to consider is title insurance.

A property that you acquire for investment purposes will transfer any interest a bank or other creditor has to you when you close on the investment. That is, you will be liable for any expenses relating to the property after the transaction is finalized.

The biggest problem is that there might be some liens on the property. These would be liens that were never revealed to you during the transaction. Sometimes a lien might be hiding within the terms of a policy and might not have been disclosed during the transaction.

This is where title insurance comes into play. This insurance policy protects you from any unexpected liens or other legal defects that might hinder your property purchase.

You must have title insurance on your investment to be safe. The problem with so many transactions is that people can quickly hide liens or even forget about them altogether. Title insurance secures you from struggling with such problems as your transaction will be covered.

What Is a Lien?

A lien is a legal right for a creditor to collect a debt from a property owner. The lien might entail some obligation for services rendered.

A lien gives a creditor the right to seize a property or other asset if the debtor does not pay it. For instance, a person who takes out a loan from a bank to pay for a home might grant a lien to the bank. The bank can assign this lien to the property.

When the homeowner does not pay the loan, the bank has the option to use the lien. The bank can seize the property and then sell it off to repay the loan. When the homeowner does pay off the entire loan, the bank will release the lien. The homeowner will then have full ownership of the property.

The terms associated with a lien can be rather complicated. It is very easy for people to lose track of liens associated with a property. This leads to concerns where a lien might appear when someone acquires a property. The worst part is that the lien might be one that the person did not anticipate. This could make it harder for a person to pay off the property.

Why Would a Lien Be Hidden?

You would think that it would be easy for liens to be made visible on any property. It is easier for liens to be hidden than you might think. A lien can be hidden attached to your property based on what a seller does or what the terms of the property are. Sometimes a lien might be hiding without a single person in the deal knowing that it actually exists. For instance:

- A seller might try and sell you a property that the person does not actually own. This could be a family member trying to sell a property that belongs to someone else who is no longer capable of handling that property.

- Homeowners might not be aware that another person could be associated with a property during the sale process. This could entail a person co-owning a property who never signed off on any transactions.

- A person could have inherited a house under the terms of a Will that is outdated. A newer edition of the Will could have intended for the real estate to be left to someone else.

- Other debts that a person owed could be linked to a property. These include liens based on tax payments, child support dues, renovation and construction costs that were never paid, etc.

There is always a chance that a lien might be discovered. This is what title insurance is for. It keeps the surprise liens from being a serious threat. With title insurance, you will only have to pay for what you know you actually owe. Any liens that were unearthed before the transaction will be owed, but any others that are discovered after the deal is made will not be a part of the transaction.

How to Get Title Insurance

It is easy to get title insurance on your new investment:

1. Contact an agent or attorney for help.

A legal authority can assist you in arranging for an insurance policy. The person you are acquiring the property from will more than likely not offer any help with this aspect.

2. The attorney or agent should contact a title insurance underwriter for the policy.

Most legal parties work with regular underwriters who understand how the legalities of real estate.

3. Review the terms associated with the policy that was drafted.

4. Review how the insurance policy can be paid.

Depending on your location, the property seller might be responsible for paying for the title insurance.

5. If you have to pay the title insurance, you must pay the appropriate one-time fee.

You might spend about $1,000 for title insurance. The cost might be higher if the value of the property is greater or the perceived risk of the investment is greater.

Title insurance is a vital part of real estate investment. Be fully aware of what can happen when finding a suitable property and that you have a sensible plan for getting the real estate without coming across any unwelcome surprises in the process.

Chapter 26: Legal Concerns

The process of acquiring or selling real estate is often complicated. You have already read about the factors that go into preparing an offer, deciding on the value of the property and so forth. There are many legal issues that have to be considered.

You don't have to be an expert in the law to be aware of the legal concerns that may develop with your property. Such legal issues might influence how you manage a property and use it.

Review the Property Valuation

The general goal is to see that the evaluation process was managed correctly and in a fair manner. Refer to the earlier chapter on property evaluation to understand the details surrounding the overall process.

Signs of a Bad Evaluation

There might be times when the evaluation appears to be unfair. Some of the signs that suggest an evaluation is not correct include the following:

- The appraiser did not consider the entire neighborhood of the property concerned.

- An appraiser might not much experience in placing values to homes.

- An appraiser could also be new to a local area and might not be familiar with a certain market.

- The property's value is dramatically different from other similar properties in an area.

- The appraiser thinks that there are certain things in a property that do not have a broad appeal as other

213

properties. These include a private pool, garages, basement development, etc.

- The general process could have been rushed and not done thoroughly.

It can be difficult to bear with a poor appraisal process. The last thing you should have to think about is if the property you want to invest in is not worth as much as what you might have hoped.

Challenging the Evaluation

You have the right to challenge the evaluation of the property if you wish. You can do this to potentially increase the value of a property you want to sell or to reduce the value of something you wish to buy.

Here are a few things you can do to challenge the valuation:

1. Provide new points of comparison.

Points of comparison, or comps, are features that show what makes a property different or the same as another property in the market. You can use comps to illustrate to an appraiser why your property is unique or why you feel the value that was imposed on it is unfair.

You can compare the real estate to others based on architectural layout, unique features inside the property, or anything else that the original appraisal process might have missed. Make sure the points of comparison you introduce are sensible.

2. Point out any existing comparisons.

Look at any comps that might be unfair. For instance, an appraiser might not incorporate home sales from the last 90 days. An appraiser could have used sales from well before then. You can show a new comparison of properties that sold just recently, thus giving you a better chance at highlighting that your building should have a more appropriate value based on what is available.

3. Highlight anything that has to be done to the property.

Sometimes the value of a property might be higher than anticipated. You might need to show the appraiser things like surfaces that need to be repaired or replaced. Be specific about anything that needs to be done to the home and why. The appraiser might change the value of the property based on what he has found out about it.

4. Look for a second opinion on your property.

You might need to hire a second appraiser to get a new value on the property. This might be the easiest thing you can do. Not all appraisers will budge based on any new information you give him about the property.

Challenging the appraisal always helps when you know there is something of interest in your property that has to be discussed. It is not always easy to convince someone about the value of a property.

Due Diligence

Due diligence is important for any investment you might be considering. Due diligence refers to the steps that must be taken to satisfy a particular legal need. You must use enough diligence to understand the property and to keep the transaction consistent and organized.

You must review your property, get the proper insurance policies, and plan the evaluation process before you purchase the property. You are expected to put in the effort to see what the property is like and that you are fully aware of what it features. Failing to put in enough due diligence into the transaction could be costly. You could foot the bill for expenses relating to problems that you were never made aware of or that you neglected to include into your plans for purchasing a property.

Review the Entire Market

The first thing to do to perform due diligence is to see what the entire market you want to invest in is like. You should spend months figuring out how the market works and what investments are available.

Review Your Financing

The financing you for your investment should be planned well in advance. Decide how much money you are willing to spend and whether or not you can afford certain financing plans. Depending on your situation, you might need to improve your credit score just to get a better deal.

You need to get plenty of bids from many people who want to help you with getting a property. Do not just stay with only one lender. Look at many banks/lenders to see what is available so you get an idea of what you can qualify for. You must review as many groups as possible so you can be assured you are getting a fair deal.

Inspect the Property

You already read about inspecting a property earlier in this guide, but it is an important point you cannot afford to ignore. You must inspect any property you wish to invest in. You will be liable for any repairs that have to be made to your property. You cannot get the value of your property adjusted in the event you find some problems after the purchase has gone through. Be sure you inspect your property to get an idea of what you will need to do and the costs involved.

Zoning

Check on the zoning rules associated with the property. This will be discussed in further detail in the next chapter. Zoning refers to what you can and cannot do with a property. A zone will be designated for specific activities based on the functions for a property in that local area. A property may be zoned for only industrial usage. The zone of another area might be strictly for residential usage, such as single homes, apartments, or duplexes.

Homeowners Associations

Review the homeowners association rules associated with what you are going to purchase. A homeowners association, or HOA, is a group run by a real estate development firm. It manages a community where many real estate properties are situated.

When you buy real estate in a certain area, you will have to join the HOA that is in charge of that area. The HOA will charge you monthly or annual fees to support the upkeep of common areas. These include the roads, the community center, landscaping, garbage pick-up, and so forth. Such fees can be a few hundred dollars every month.

An HOA might also include rules for what you can and cannot do to your investment. You might be limited to what you can do to the exterior, fencing, or restrict you from renting your property to a third-person. The rules can vary. You must research information on any HOA in existence where you want to invest. This part of due diligence ensures you have a full understanding of what you can expect.

Title Insurance

Do not forget about the title insurance for your property. This part of due diligence, as mentioned earlier, protects you from any outstanding liens that might be hiding within your transaction. The title insurance policy ensures you will not be subjected to anything illegal. It should not cost much when compared with the total value of your investment.

Evaluate the Financial Risk

Every investment has a financial risk to it. This is definitely the case with real estate. With something worth hundreds of thousands of dollars or even millions, you could always be at risk of losing what you have invested. You must look at what you are doing with your investment above all else.

Check the pricing points for the real estate you are interested in buying. Analyze the price based on factors, such as how property values have changed in a local area and what unique points about the property.

Every property has its own particular risk. There is no such thing as a guaranteed profit in any investment. The values of real estate can increase with inflation, but they could also crash depending on things like foreclosures in an area or land depreciation. Be prepared to consider what can happen in any place that you want to invest in.

Liability Considerations

You could be held liable for any problems that might develop on your property. For instance, you might own a rental home and what happens if someone gets injured on your property? Sometimes the person who is hurt will be liable because of some illegal action. In other cases, you could be liable because you were unable to maintain your property as well as you should have.

You have to keep the property maintained well to ensure no one is hurt. You could be sued if the property was not maintained appropriately and someone was injured. A property management team can help with maintaining your property, but you would be liable for whatever that team does and how well it can work for you.

The environmental risks in an area have to be considered too. These risks often involve things like tornadoes, hurricanes, earthquakes, and other common natural disasters. These are problems that can threaten the stability of a property. While you might not be liable for damages relating to these disasters, you should still have liability insurance on your property to ensure you are covered for losses due to any of those issues.

The liability issues will vary based on the area. Some liabilities you cannot control while others are ones you can manage yourself. Check each concern about a property to get an idea of what could cause you a loss on your investment. This is to also give you peace of mind when acquiring an investment property.

Commercial Liability Considerations

Any commercial properties you want to invest in should be explored in detail. You have to review any party that plans on conducting business within your commercial property. For instance, you could review every tenant that comes into a property to see what one does and how it might operate.

There is always the chance that the commercial tenants of a property might engage in illegal activities. A business could be a front for an illegal drug trade or human trafficking ring, for instance. Maybe a business could engage in actions that support terror-related organizations. Others might store things they have stolen or acquired illegally on a site.

Make sure any tenants are properly vetted, and that you have a plan on hand for taking care of any issues that might arise. You may be liable for any problems that take place on your property due to a business entity engaging in dangerous and potentially illegal activities. You can read information in a later chapter about how to vet possible tenants.

Be prepared to consider the many legal aspects that come with owning real estate.

Chapter 27: Zoning Rules

A very specific part of the legal aspects of real estate investing is the zoning rules of a property. Every property is subjected to zoning laws. A zone will determine the types of buildings that are allowed to be built in an area. The zoning laws in an area are critical to helping you understand what you can utilize when investing in a property. More importantly, they keep communities organized.

You would not want to have a residential property near some huge industrial manufacturing plant. This is where zones come into play. They are planned to keep certain properties away from others and to create areas that are safe for residential use.

You must consider zoning rules if you want to build a new structure. This is vital for when you want to buy land. You must think about the zone the property is in and that you have a good plan for how people can use it based on the zoning rules that have been put into place.

What Are Zones?

Zoning regulations stipulate what a certain property can be used for and what can be placed on the plots of land. A zone provides the rules and standards that properties have to meet. A commercial property can be developed on a commercial plot while a single-family home would be situated in a residential zone.

Zones have been used since 1916 when New York City established the first-ever zoning laws in the United States. Those laws were established to improve the quality of life in the city and to ensure workplaces and homes could be separated. Such laws ensure that people will not be subjected to difficult conditions in their home areas. Every city or regional area will have its own zones; local governments are responsible for deciding how the entire area is zoned.

What Restrictions Can Be Put into Place?

You can always choose to buy land that you can build new properties on. However, you have to follow the restrictions that are imposed on a certain zone. Zoning rules are established to ensure that people do not use certain areas for purposes outside of what local authorities want people to use them for.

Some of the more common restrictions you might come across on a zone include rules about:

- How a property can be built; this includes rules on the architectural features of a building, whether it is a one-story, two-story, or multi-level building.

- Where utility lines may be located.

- How any accessory buildings can be built.

- How large certain buildings might be; you might have limits on how tall or wide a building can be on a particular lot.

- The total number of rooms in a single building.

Every zone has its own rules for what you can and cannot incorporate into that property. Be sure to look at the rules relating to a property zone and that you follow them if you ever plan on buying a property.

Types of Zoning

Some properties will be covered by their own individual zones. There are a few specific types of zones that you must look into that go well beyond some of the basics. Each zone has its own intricacies that should be investigated. These go well beyond the types of properties that can be utilized in a certain zone. You must look into these points if you wish to buy a plot of land and you want to add something new to it.

Residential

A residential zone is for properties for people to live in. These include single-family homes, apartment buildings or any other space designed for everyday living. Even a trailer park can be considered residential zone. The permanence of some homes makes the process of determining which zones can be residential somewhat complicated.

Residential zoning rules often have limits on what can be built. Although any home for a permanent residence can be used in a residential zone, there might be rules over how many animals can be kept on a property. Typical domestic pets like cats, dogs, birds, small reptiles, and fish are allowed to be in a residential zone. There might be rules as to whether people can keep horses, cows, chickens, sheep, pigs, and other in a residential area.

Some rules can also be imposed as to how many residential properties can be situated in an area at a given time. A certain limit might ensure there is enough room for all of the people within a certain zone. There might also be rules on mobile homes. A mobile home could be allowed to stay within a zone for a few days, but it might not be used as a long-term home.

Some rules may be imposed as to what businesses can operate out of a home in a residential zone. Home-based businesses can be utilized in a residential property in most cases.

Considering how the work-at-home revolution has been spreading over the years, it is not hard for people to set up offices in their homes. There might be rules as to what types of businesses can be set up. These include rules relating to:

- Signage; any signs that could be used might be minimal or not allowed at all.

- Noise concerns; a home business must not create noise to where other property owners might be disrupted or bothered.

- Whether employees come from outside the residential zone into the property.

- Any instances where people may be invited to a property; a place that regularly entertains physical customers might not be allowed.

- Parking rules; there might be strict limits on how roads near some properties can be used and what kinds of vehicles are allowed to park.

- Any separate entrance facilities regardless of whether they are attached to the main property or not.

Commercial

A commercial zoning focuses on properties that would be used for commercial intentions. You could set up an office building, a shopping center, a hotel, nightclub, restaurant, or any other place designed to serve commercial needs on one of these properties. The key is that the property in question would be used to create income by serving the needs that people in a community might have.

Commercial zones are popular in that the vacant land on those zones can be built upon depending on what the rules for development are in those areas. The opportunities are almost endless when it comes to what can be done with a commercial plot.

Even some residential properties could be placed in a commercial zone. Apartment or condominium buildings can be added in a zone in some instances. This is thanks to how they help businesses to raise money from rent. The fact that some condo buildings might include a few commercial entities on the first or second floors helps too. Of course, single-family homes are not eligible to be placed on a commercial plot.

While many kinds of businesses can work on a commercial plot, there are often exceptions. In particular, adult entertainment establishments might be outlawed on some plots. These include billiard halls, bars that focus exclusively on alcohol, craft beer breweries, tobacco shops, wine cellars or adult movie or toy shops. Some commercial plots will happily take in those types of adult-oriented businesses, but those plots would have to be in areas that families or minors are not likely to visit.

There might also be rules as to what types of businesses can be situated near schools or churches. A commercial plot within a certain distance of a school or church might not be allowed - a restaurant that serves alcoholic beverages, for instance. The laws can vary. Check on any limits on what can be placed on a commercial plot before you consider investing. This could directly influence your decision based on the types of businesses that you are willing to have on your property.

Accessory Subsections

Some commercial properties can utilize accessory subsections. These work as places where people can apply for an exception to engage in certain actions. For instance, a hotel in an area where bars might not be allowed could apply for the right to set up its own bar. This would mean that the bar could be used in the property provided it is a part of the hotel. Businesses themselves would have to review what they can do in these areas to determine if the property can qualify for such accessory functions.

Industrial

Industrial zones are good for manufacturing plants, research and development buildings, warehouses and other industrial businesses. Many industrial zones are kept in areas far from residential and commercial pots. This is due to the noises that might be produced in some areas, the risk of hazardous materials in some sites, and so forth. There might still be rules in some of these zones over what can be incorporated on a site.

Some industrial zones might be geographically larger in size than other zones. This is due to some industrial buildings needing more space for them to work properly. The extensive amount of work that comes with getting such a property ready can be extensive and often a challenge to manage.

Agricultural

An agricultural zone is a place that concentrates on farming functions. These are places that concentrate on growing and raising food that can be used with commercial intentions in mind. In most cases, an agricultural zone might include a space for growing fruits and vegetables. It may also be a place for raising animals that can be used for meat, eggs, milk, and other products that they might produce. Many agricultural zones are large in size as a means of allowing enough room to grow foods in or to accommodate animals.

Agricultural zones are made to create areas where farming businesses can be fully protected from residential encroachment.

Such a zone is also vital for distinguishing which properties are eligible to take advantage of governmental programs and incentives. Properties in agricultural zones may be eligible to receive tax benefits or to get subsidies from the government. These are provided to farmers to help keep them afloat and to encourage various activities that keep the national economy running.

Rural

A rural zone is focused more on a ranch or farm. It is used to cover a more recreational type of farm area that is not designed with commercial intentions. It could be a place that people can visit, but any commercial actions that take place in a rural area would be minimal at best. A rural zone should be large in geographic area and will cover areas where horses or cattle might be found. Any building that works for a ranch or farm could be eligible to be placed on a rural plot.

Historic

Some zones are historic properties include significant restrictions on what people can do with the properties. A historic zone is one that is deemed by an organization like the National Register of Historic Places to be critical to the history of a local area. It could be a place where a historical figure lived or where a very important event took place in the past.

You may be limited as to what you could do with a property in a historic zone. You might not be allowed to modify the physical layout or floor plan of a property. The area would have to be preserved in a certain condition to reflect the history.

You might still get some allowances from the government or another entity for maintaining and repairing a historic property. This is provided that the property is restored or refurbished to its historic status. It is fine to repair a place to keep it sturdy and less likely to deteriorate, but you are not permitted to add new things to a property to make it more interesting to people.

Historic zones are typically small in area. Sometimes a zone might be limited to just one block or individual property. In other cases, a zone might cover an entire area. The Fells Point region in Baltimore or Laclede's Landing section of St. Louis are good examples of historic zones. Although people can set up their businesses in those regions, they would have to do this within severe limits over what can be done and how a property can be organized and run.

Aesthetic

Aesthetic zones have become more commonplace in recent years. Many high-end commercial and residential properties can incorporate their own aesthetic zones. This is a zone that includes things that add to the functionality or appearance of a larger zone. An aesthetic zone may be reserved for things like a solar panel array, a series of satellite dishes, a large landscape, or fountain layout, a fence or even an outdoor deck. If the item in question can be organized with a beautiful display, it can be a part of an aesthetic zone. A local review committee would have analyzed it to see if the property can be called aesthetic.

Combination

Combination zoning can be found in some places. You might find areas that can handle both residential and commercial properties. These zones will have their own rules for what can be done in a certain area.

All of these zones are different based on what you can and cannot do. You must look at what can work in these areas if you ever plan on investing in land or property anywhere. Such rules are interesting and worth looking into.

Challenging a Zoning Rule

You might have an interest in a certain area and want to acquire a property that you would use for a particular intention. You might acquire a large building and want to use it as a commercial office complex to allow many businesses to use it. Maybe that building is on land that does not allow commercial properties like an office building. What would you do?

You can always look for an office building in an area that is actually designated for commercial properties. You can choose to challenge the zoning regulations in a certain area.

You can contact a local government office in the area that covers your property. You can petition a challenge to the zoning laws in an area in which you want to establish a business. To do this, you must have all your plans for zoning set up in writing. This includes information on the type of property you want to utilize, where you want to place it (or where it now exists), and your general intention for it.

The party you would contact for challenging a zoning rule will vary by region. Sometimes a city government is responsible for determining the zones. In other cases, a state or county government might determine the zones. Check on the rules in your area.

You would also have to explain why you feel the zoning rules in an area are unfair. You must be reasonable in your arguments. Sometimes you might make a point if the property you want to set up could be to the economic benefit of an area. You might also argue that your plans would not disrupt actions in other properties. Whatever the case is, you would have to be realistic and sensible in your argument to let people know why your plans are viable and useful.

Alternative Options to a Challenge

You do not always have to challenge zoning laws. You can choose one of many alternatives to allow you to have a certain investment in a zone that it might not normally be allowed. These alternative options include the following choices.

Conditional Use Permit

A conditional use permit can be acquired from the local government. This is to allow you to use a property for some intention while ensuring the impact on a local area is kept to a minimum. For instance, you could set up a small commercial property like a diner at the bottom level of a larger condo building in a residential zone. This might be organized with a layout that is consistent with the rest of the building and does not obstruct traffic or architectural features in any way.

Amendment

An amendment is an additional rule of local zoning laws. The amendment might expand upon the things that can be done in a certain property. For instance, residential property might be allowed to have smaller commercial space on the ground floor. Amendments can be established provided they can show some kind of benefit to investors or residents in an area. These can make it easier for a property to be more valuable, but a local government board would have to certify the amendment before it can be enacted. There are no guarantees that such a rule could be added.

Variance

A variance can be utilized if you have a plan for a certain area and not getting that plan approved would result in some kind of hardship. This might entail some issue where a business or other special plan cannot work properly. For instance, you might prove that a business you are investing in will struggle if it cannot operate in a certain zone. A variance can be a useful, but it might be a challenge to actually get this to work for you.

Be aware of the zoning rules that come affect any property you wish to invest in. You must watch for this if you want to buy land for future real estate investment in particular. While you have the option to get some adjustments made to local zoning rules, there are no guarantees that you can get those changes to work for you.

Chapter 28: Tax Advantages

Real estate investing is intriguing due to the versatility and diversity of the field. The possible profits you can realize from of your investments will add to what makes it a great field to enter into. Did you know that you could also take advantage of some outstanding tax benefits?

There are several tax benefits that apply to investing and holding real estate. These can reduce your tax burdens associated.

Some of these benefits will work while you own a property. Other benefits might not apply until after you sell your property. It makes sense to see what the tax advantages for your investment plans can be.

Note: The tax advantages listed here are good for United States residents. The rules may vary based on the country your property is in.

Capital Gains Tax

The capital gains tax is a tax applied to any profits you make from the sale of an investment. The profit has to be significant so that the value of the property as you sell it is higher than it was when you bought it.

The capital gains tax entails the following:

1. The sale price is calculated.

2. The sale costs associated with the property are deducted.

3. The original purchase price is then deducted.

4. Any costs relating to improvements on your property should be calculated and deducted from the total.

5. Any depreciation that you claimed on the property must also be deducted.

Here's an example of a capital gains tax:

1. You could buy a home for $400,000. This total may include legal fees and some fees for your loan.

2. You could sell that home for $700,000 a few years later. This would give you a profit of $300,000.

3. You might pay a real estate commission of $30,000 on the sale price. This cuts the total gains down to $270,000.

4. The value of the improvements you made would then be calculated. If you spent $40,000 on improvements, the gains will decrease to $230,000.

5. You could have claimed about $30,000 in depreciation over time. The gains would go up to $260,000.

6. The $260,000 in capital gains would be taxed based on an appropriate rate.

The tax rate will be 15 percent. Therefore, you would have to pay $39,000 as the capital gains tax.

The tax rate will vary based on the situation:

- You could pay no capital gains tax if the profit on your real estate was small. People who earn less than $38,000 should not have to pay a capital gains tax.

- A tax of 15 percent applies to people who make profits up to about $400,000.

- The maximum capital gains tax is 20 percent. This is for people who earn $425,000 or more.

- The threshold for how much you would spend is higher if you are married and are filing a joint return. A single person can realize up to $38,600 in gains tax-free, but a married couple filing jointly can realize up to $77,200 tax-free.

Married Couple Concerns

The capital gains tax is significantly higher for married couples where the two people file separately than it is for a couple that files jointly. A married couple filing separately must pay 20 percent in capital gains tax for gains of $239,501 or more. This threshold is significantly lower than what any other person might spend on the tax. In other words, a married couple looking to invest in real estate should file jointly to ensure the tax rate is lower.

There is an option that a married couple or a single person can use to avoid having to pay the capital gains tax, and this is deferred tax.

Deferring the Capital Gains Tax

The capital gains tax can be frustrating but that does not mean you have to struggle with it. You can defer the capital gains tax by moving the gains that you earned into another home that you want to invest in.

According to Section 1031 of the IRS Code, you can sell your real estate investment and then use the profits to invest in another property. The property in question must be similar to the original property that you sold.

However, you must have a third-party hold your profits before you complete the purchase of the new investment property. You will have to pay the capital gains tax if you take out that money.

This tax benefit makes it easy for you to get more out of an investment. You can use the money you have earned to continue working in the real estate field. Section 1031 encourages further investing and can make a real difference in your plans.

Installment Sale

Another tax benefit to look into is the installment sale. This is similar to the capital gains tax deferment plan as it allows you to keep from having to pay that tax. An installment sale requires a unique process.

In an installment sale, at least one payment on a loan will be sent after the taxable year closes. This allows the taxes on any capital gains to be deferred to a future year. Regular payments or installments must be made on the property for this to work. This allows you to keep from having to pay taxes sooner.

Living In a Property You are Flipping

One of the main things you can do to avoid paying taxes is to consider living in a property that you want to flip. While it can take a while to restore a property you wish to flip, you can still keep from having to pay taxes on the profits relating to that property.

To take advantage of this, you would have to do the following:

1. After acquiring a property that you wish to flip, you would have to move into the property.

The property you are flipping should be listed as your primary residence.

2. You must also properly live in that property for two of the next five years.

3. After selling the property, you will be able to get a tax-free profit on the property you sell.

The maximum coverage you can get is up to $250,000 in profits without taxes as a single individual or $500,000 if you are part of a couple living in the same property. You may be subjected to taxes if you get any profits greater than that.

Depreciation Expenses

You may be able to get depreciation expenses cleared off your taxes. The taxable income on your investment refers to the rental income you earn minus the depreciation expenses involved. Therefore, the taxes will be reduced if the value of your property declines in some way. This includes declines in a home's value due to age or use or from declines in the value of the land the home is on. This is a great benefit, but you would have to review your property value regularly to see if any depreciation has occurred on it. You can apply to get this tax benefit if the depreciation you are suspecting has actually happened.

No Taxes on Appreciation

Another benefit involves not having to pay taxes on the appreciation of your property's value. The cost that you are taxed on is based on the money that you actually spent on buying a property. You will not be charged extra because the value is going up on your investment.

Leaving your property to your heirs will reset the appreciation tax threshold. The new tax rate will be based on the property value after all that appreciation is applied. Any new appreciation that your heirs will receive will not be taxed. This is a point that will be covered later.

Chapter 29: Market Signs (Both Positive and Negative)

Every investment market has its own signs for how a market is evolving. The real estate market is no different. The signs associated with what can happen within the real estate market are distinct and can help you understand what might happen with an investment you are interested in.

Knowing how the market is changing and evolving can help you see when the right times for investing might happen. Having a clear idea of what is happening in the market is vital to your investment success.

While there are many signs suggesting that a property's value is going to increase, there are also many risks that might suggest a value will decline. These points are critical to understand as they can make real long-term changes in the values of properties.

Note: Although these are all good signs to look into, there are no guarantees that a property value in a local area will actually increase or decrease based on things that take place in that region. Every market you can invest in is unique. The points here are simple guidelines for you to consider.

How to Tell if a Property's Value Is Going to Increase

There are many good signs to watch for when looking at properties but these signs are not guarantees necessarily that the value of a property is actually going to increase. Be on the lookout for properties with these signs:

- The values of properties in a local area might be increasing.

- New construction is happening.

- The foreclosure rate in an area is declining.

- Roads in an area are being built to help make a local area more accessible.

- Mortgages in a local area are being paid off.

- New businesses are looking to bring in jobs in a local area.

- Public transportation services are becoming more commonplace in a local area. This could be even more beneficial if this was light rail services rather than just standard bus services.

The point is that new construction and improved conditions in a local area might make it easier for properties to start increasing in value. You might want to check on the histories of any of these properties. This is just to get an idea of how the value has changed.

How to Tell a Property's Value Will Decrease

There are numerous signs that suggest that a property's value is apt to decline. These problems are serious risks that must be considered:

- Stores are closing or are moving from one place to another area.

- Property taxes might start to increase.

- Individual properties are being converted. A house might be converted into a duplex or into several apartments.

- A mall, shopping center, or other large commercial space in an area might have lost a prominent tenant. For instance, a property near a mall that just lost a Macy's or Sears could hurt because it is an indication of decline.

- Public transportation services in an area are being scaled back. These include stations closing or schedules for service not being as busy as they used to be.

- Public spaces are not being maintained well.

All of these points for how property values can increase or decrease are important to explore.

Corporations Relocating (In and Out)

One of the main reasons why so many places around the country try to lure businesses is such businesses can help to improve the local economy. When Amazon announced that it would open a second headquarters and would start taking in candidates for that area in late 2017, many cities around the United States started planning their own efforts to bring Amazon to their areas. They knew that with Amazon coming in, it would be easier for a region to get more jobs and therefore increase the financial stability of an area.

There is a real estate-related benefit that comes with this. When more jobs come into an area through large corporations, it becomes attractive for people to want to relocate to the area. This, in turn, makes properties more in demand. The potential for new construction to start new buildings is strong too. The point is that when more work and business opportunities come into an area, people will want to move there.

New Construction Work

When new construction projects are started, a shift in the properties in an area will start to develop. This suggests that people are going to want to move into a local area. It may also be the sign that new commercial projects might be developed as well. The general interest that the public might have will increase. Some people who are looking for homes might be interested in finding newer properties rather than older ones.

New road construction can make a difference too. The area will become more accessible when new roads are built. This could potentially increase the values of properties. People will want to move into the area when they know they can travel from home to work with ease. This could be not only new roads and highways but also rail services being developed in the area.

It might take some time for the new construction to be a benefit to an area. Sometimes it might take a while for the values of properties to go increase because it could take months or years for all the new properties in an area to be fully occupied. Of course, many real estate developers and agents will try to sell these properties to people while they are being built, thus reducing the potential for them to be vacant after they are fully constructed. This could help to keep the values of properties from being depressed due to local vacancies.

Some properties might experience temporary declines in their values due to all the construction. Those properties might not be easily accessible or could bear with excessive noises or traffic issues from construction equipment and employees. You might need to wait to see how far a property's price will drop due to local construction before you actually invest in it.

Can Problems Also Develop Due to Construction?

As exciting as new construction can be, there are some cases where substantial problems might develop in an area due to all the construction. Some of the more common issues people should be aware of when finding a property include the following:

- The soil in an area might start to erode. This could cause some surfaces in an area to weaken.

- Pollutants produced during the construction might potentially impact the air quality in an area.

- Sometimes the added traffic in an area can cause air pollution to become even more prominent. The traffic might make it hard for people to move on some roads. Some places might be noisy too.

- The water quality in an area might be harmed due to pollution in an area and the erosion of soil.

Not all areas will be negatively impacted by construction projects. There is still potential for some issues to develop in an area under contruction.

Millennials May Help

People have been talking quite a bit about millennials. These are people that became adults during the early part of the 21st Century. People have various ideas as to when millennials were born, but it is safe to say they were born in the early or mid-1980s for the most part.

Millennials have been the butt of many jokes about society and how it is changing. One thing for certain is that they are becoming more powerful and influential than ever before. This is important to the real estate market as they are the people who are likely to buy properties these days. These people are spending money on various types of properties including traditional homes and smaller condos.

You can tell that the market in a local area might change based on the number of millennials that are relocating to a local area. Specifically, millennials might be looking for properties that are a little cheaper. Millennials, on average, have less disposable income to work with.

Millennials these days have lots of debts to deal with. These include debts relating to various loans they might have, health insurance charges, education loans, and expenses relating to any jobs they have. These people are looking to keep their funds under control. As a result, millennials are looking for rental properties with smaller rents or home loans with lower monthly payments. They want to keep the added burden of real estate expenses from being beyond their financial status.

This could impact the real estate market in many ways. It might keep you from getting as much money in rent as you might wish. As millennials remain cautious about how they spend money on real estate and rent, it might be easy for a property to go up in value. This is thanks to those people working hard to keep from getting into foreclosures or other issues.

Check on the demographics of an area you want to invest in. Look at if millennials are being attracted to a local area. These people might directly influence your choice of investment. More millennials in an area could be a sign that the values of properties in an area are possibly increasing. They could also be a sign that rents are going to decrease.

Foot Traffic

One sign that a market is growing in size is people in an area being willing to do things in public. People are often willing to get out there and have fun in their communities and even get to know others in an area. That is one of the best things about many local communities. They are places that people will get to know each other in and enjoy living in because they know all the people who are living there. It is a truly unique thing about life that anyone could appreciate.

Properties are often worth more in areas that has plenty of foot traffic. This includes foot traffic in many forms:

- People might walk from their properties to their places of work instead of taking their cars.

- People could also be on the streets for their daily walks. These include walks on their own or with other friends. Some people might walk their dogs too.

- Children could be out on the street playing around. They could be playing various sports on the streets with one another.

A place that has enough people on the streets is often perceived as being a little safer. It suggests that people are willing to get out there and enjoy life outdoors. A neighborhood that is considered to be safer thanks to foot traffic might have a better value.

Meanwhile, an area where there are hardly any people outdoors could be seen as a quiet area where people are afraid to get out and do things. This could suggest that a region is too dangerous. It becomes easy for people to feel worried when others in an area are not out and about and being with each other.

Public Space Considerations

Many public spaces in a local area can make a direct impact on the values of properties in a local area. These include open parks, ball parks, tennis areas, playgrounds, and skateboard parks, fountains and other artistic flourishes in an area.

Sometimes the values of properties can increase if there are better public spaces. When a new public area is introduced in a region, the space will have a newer and more unique look to it. This could help to increase the total value of a property.

Some public areas might create more inviting spaces for people to visit. An open park can be a place where community events are held. It could be inviting for picnics, weekend markets, and other things.

Over time, public spaces might become dangerous if they are not be maintained well. A park might look uncared for. A public fountain could stop working. Maybe some trees in an area have grown to where they could break apart or fall over in a wind. Any public area that has not been maintained could end up being dangerous. It could be a place where illegal criminal activities could take place.

Look and see how the public spaces are arranged and that they look inviting or interesting to you. It will be easier for you to invest in a place if you can find that it is not dangerous or unappealing in its layout or arrangement.

Who Else Is Moving In?

There are many other groups beyond just millennials and businesses that might impact how property values can change. What other parties might be moving into the area you are interested in? Sometimes the changing demographics can make a difference as older groups move and newer ones that are more dynamic and interesting:

- People who have more income might impact the values of properties in an area.

There is always a chance for property values to increase when people who earn more money on average move into a region. Those people are more likely to have better credit ratings and less likely to get into foreclosures or other problems with paying for their properties.

- Trendy businesses might move into an area.

Not all businesses have to be huge to drive up property values. A trendy business like a fancy restaurant or a popular retail chain could improve property values. Even a supermarket could make an impact. A high-end spot retailer like Wegmans or Publix or an organic market like Sprouts or Whole Foods might be more valuable than the average Kroger, Safeway or Harris Teeter.

For Rent Signs

There are many properties in any area that might be for rent. You can always benefit from properties for rent when you buy them. There is such a thing as having too many for rent signs.

A local area might not be popular if there are too many for rent signs in an area. Properties might decline in value due to fewer properties being owned by others in an area. The lack of long-term tenants might be a real problem. It could suggest a lack of stability in an area, thus making it harder for properties to increase in value.

When people start moving out of an area, it becomes harder for properties to increase in value. People might feel as though no one is truly committed to the local area. The risk of properties falling into disrepair will increase. This, in turn, causes values to decline.

Look for the number of for rent or sale signs in an area. If an area has lots of these signs it may not be appealing because of the lack of interest that people have in a region, let alone no real long-term interest in staying.

School Quality

Properties that are located near schools are often worth more. People love to find properties that are close to schools as it is more convenient for families with children. The perceived safety and community benefits of a school in a local area can cause a positive impact on the local area.

A school could be a detriment to property values if the school becomes unpopular and fewer students are attending. There are many reasons why a school's attendance totals might start to decline:

- Fewer families are in a local area, thus resulting in fewer children attending a school.

- Some people in neighborhood might not be interested in starting families or are past the age of raising children.

- People are moving their children out to different schools. They might do so because they think certain schools in an area might not be good enough.

- Homeschooling has become more popular in recent time. Parents might take their children out of traditional schools and homeschool them. They might do this for philosophical or religious reasons, but some may feel they can do better than the schools.

There are also times when the quality of services at a school might weaken. These could include problems like:

- The funding for services in a school could start to decline. This might suggest that the services at a school are not as good as they should be.

- Classroom sizes might be too large. It is harder for students to get personal attention when the average class sizes are too large. This hurts the overall quality of a school.

- Test scores might reflect the quality of a school. Standardized testing results could cause a school to become unpopular.

These are all legitimate concerns to be aware of. When a school starts to struggle and becomes less popular or prestigious, the values of properties in the area start to decline. Find out whether services in a local area are adequate or if they are struggling to provide students with the proper education.

The Value of the Hospital

A hospital will help to increase the values of properties in an area. People feel more comfortable when they know that there are medical services in the local area that they can trust. This is especially important when it comes to emergencies. Living in an area close to a hospital is important, especially to people who are older or have significant health issues.

Property values will increase when a hospital is close and those values will decline when a hospital closes.

What is even worse is that the businesses in a local area could also close or decide to move. These include businesses that are often near hospitals for convenience. For instance, a florist that is based near a hospital might move to the new location close to where the hospital has relocated. Other businesses might start to close as the local region becomes less popular.

Find information on the medical health services and other businesses in a local area. See if anything has closed recently. This will give an indication if there is a potential for properties in an area to become less popular for whatever reason.

Chapter 30: Sales Analysis Report

The next point of real estate investing to take a closer look at is the sales analysis report. This is a special type of report that will help you understand what is happening to a property's value. You can use this to understand why the value of a property is changing.

Real estate agents and others associated with the industry will work hard to identify many points related to the market. The chances for the sales totals in a property to change and shift need to be investigated. A sales analysis report will help you understand how market prices are determined.

Where Can You Get a Report?

A sales analysis report can be gathered by a local real estate agent, but you could also check online to see what information is available about a property. A website like realtor.com can provide you with detailed information on any property.

You might need to get multiple reports. These include individual reports for multiple properties in an area. These reports should help you with decide on what property to purchase. You could even get an idea of any trends in a local area. Getting as much information on a market as possible is vital to your investment success.

Demand For a Property

One part of a sales analysis report involves the demand for a property. The demand refers to how many people have been looking into a certain property. You can tell if a local region is becoming very popular based on the demand indicated.

A sales analysis report can review what the demand is and point out concerns with it. There might be a long-term increase or decrease in sales, for example. A long-term trend might indicate that there is either a problem with a market or that the potential for growth might be strong.

Finding a decline in the demand for property in a report can be critical to understanding what is happening in a market. A decline might suggest that there are concerns in a local neighborhood that are keeping people from being interested. Sometimes it might imply that people are moving toward other regions to invest. It will indicate why the sales are trending down.

When there is an increase in interest, you might have to spend more or put in a more aggressive campaign to buy a property in that particular area.

Analysis of Expired Listings

Many markets have information on expired listings. These details will help you to identify properties that were once available on the market. Those properties could have been made available but were pulled off the market for a time because no one was buying them. This could be a sign that there is a problem with a property. There are many good reasons for why a property's listing could have expired:

- A property might not have been easily accessible.

- A building might not be in the best possible condition. Customers might have found it to be either too dangerous or maybe too expensive to repair and maintain.

- A property could also have been priced too high when compared with other similar properties in an area.

- The features of a property might not have been interesting to some investors.

Who Is Buying Property?

A sales analysis report can include details on the types of people who are buying real estate. However, the information would be more generic or broad in nature. The report will not be specific in terms of who is buying real estate. It would not include the names of individual groups or people.

Rather, the report has information on certain demographics. These include:

- Where a person is from.

- How much money that person holds.

- Whether the person is part of a larger investment group.

- The general intentions that someone has for buying a property.

The sales analysis process will indicate how much revenue is coming from people in certain demographics or from particular geographic areas. It helps to understand the types of people who are more interested in a property.

More importantly, this gives information on who are regular clients. You might notice in a report that the people investing in properties are coming from the same places. These could be the same people working on investments in a certain area.

The information can also identify how well marketing and advertising efforts are working. This is for real estate service providers that are trying to market their properties to specific groups of people. Sometimes a marketing campaign might focus on people within certain industries or income levels. The report will show if the campaign is actually reaching those people and serving them properly.

All of the points listed in the sales analysis report are vital to the success of your real estate investment plans. You must use this report to get a clear idea of what something is worth and how it got to that point.

There are a few parts of the sales analysis report that are especially important for your investment success. The next three chapters are all about specific aspects of the report that you really have to focus on to get an idea of what makes a property worth the asking price.

Chapter 31: Estimates

This chapter is all about a very specific point relating to a sales analysis report that is so important it deserves its own section. The estimates that are found in a real estate property are important to explore when looking into what is available on the market and more importantly, it gives you an idea of why a property has a certain value.

A sales analysis report will estimate the prices of properties on the market. In most cases, you can get an analysis from a real estate agent or another group that represents a person who is trying to sell a property. Contacting a seller's agent might help to give you an idea of what a property may be worth today.

The estimate itself shows a very specific value, but you will get more than just that total. You will also get information on why that property has the value.

The estimate is not intended to be the official price of the property. The estimate just helps you to guide your offers and to give you a rough idea of what the property is worth. This chapter does give a good idea for what to expect out of one.

Past Values

When you look at the information about a property, you will get details on many values:

- The original value of the home when it was first put on the market after being built.

- The value that a person might have sold the property for in the past; this is provided someone else has lived in it and sold it.

- Any evaluations that have been made; these include cases where an evaluation was made after significant modifications or repairs to a property.

- Any differences between what someone sold a property for before and what it is listed for now.

Every property has its own individual price history. Make sure you know how those values have changed over time.

Local Sales

An estimate may also be based on local sales in an area. These sales are for properties that are similar. Sometimes these sales will directly impact the estimate to create a fair playing field in the market. These also give a clue to if people are actually demanding real estate in an area.

Specific Features of Properties

Every property in the real estate market has its own unique qualities. Sometimes the specific features of a property might be worth more in the estimate. For instance:

- A home with an artificial turf lawn might be more attractive in the southwest where it is difficult to grow natural grass. It would be worth more there than it would be in other markets.

- A property with a private basketball court or tennis court would surely be more valuable if that space is in a community that does not have any such courts nearby.

- Properties with larger garages might be more valuable if there are more roads located in an area. These include both rough roads for SUVs or highways.

- A fireplace would be valuable if the property is in an area that can get cold. This includes properties in the northern part of the country.

- A swimming pool might be appealing, but it could be worth even more if it is a below-ground pool.

Every estimator has his own value attached to certain features of a property. He might not value a pool or a tennis court. Getting several estimates on a property is always a good idea.

Commercial Operations

Sometimes the estimates will be based on some of the commercial operations that can take place on a site. The type of commercial function that a property is designed for can make a real difference. While any office building could host all sorts of businesses that cater to different types of people, some commercial sites might have specific needs in mind.

Some buildings might be designed specifically for medical and health-related services. These include buildings that can house dental services offices, chiropractic firms, psychiatry services and much more. A health-related property could be worth more thanks to the ongoing demand that people will have for various health services. The diversity of a property is what could make a property more valuable.

A building that focuses on educational services could be worth more on the market. A property might serve as a continuing education center. It might also be a place for preschool education or for helping people who have learning difficulties.

While a property might be designed with a specific commercial need in mind that does not mean that property must be used with that intention. A place that is made for housing educational functions or school-related activities could be converted into an office building, for instance. It is often best to use a property for whatever intention it was made for in the first place. An estimate will tell you what a property is designed for so you can determine which tenants might fit in perfectly in that area. This could also help you figure out who you should be marketing a space to.

Is This the Official Price?

Although the information that is provided by an estimate can be useful, you should not assume that the estimate is definitely going to be the final price you would spend on a property. There are always going to be some kind of variance between what the estimate of a property is and what the actual value is.

Keep a variance of about 5 percent for the estimate. That is, the actual value of the property could be 5 percent higher or lower in value than what the estimate states. This variance can help you determine what might be required for the purchase. You can also use this information in the negotiation process.

The estimate is just the suggestion. There is always a chance that the value could change quickly for a number of reasons.

What Can You Use Online?

You have the option to use one of the various online tools to help you determine an estimate for a property you want to buy. For instance:

- Zillow is a popular website that offers an estimate tool that has inspired many other real estate sites to create similar programs. The Zillow tool is used to determine the proper values, or Zestimates, of properties that are listed on that site.

- Redfin also has an estimate tool that reviews general comps that may be used to determine a property's value.

- Chase has information on local trends and the values of homes that sold recently in a local area. These are factored heavily into the estimates that the proper lending service provider offers.

- ForSaleByOwner.com also has a Pricing Scout program that gives you a full analysis of the local market and a review of recent trends in the area. This also gives you full information on comparable properties in a local area. You have to register for the site to actually use it.

These online tools are not intended to give you the exact value of a property in a given area. There are many other options to choose from, but the ones listed above are generally considered to be the most popular options that people use.

The estimates that you come across when finding a property should always be reviewed. A sales analysis report will help you understand what you might expect from your investment.

Chapter 32: Actual Sales vs. Projected Sales

One point you will notice in a sales analysis report is the actual sales of properties in a region and the projections for that area. By reviewing these, you will get a clear idea of what the demand for properties in a region might be. This gives you information on the estimates or if there is a problem with properties in a certain region.

This is a useful measurement that is often utilized in many lines of work and not just in the real estate field. While anyone can make an estimate of what something might be worth or what it could sell for, that estimate will never be prefect. Your sales analysis report should inform you about the actual sales have changed when compared with the projected sales that were available at the time of the sales.

Actual Sales in An Area

A sales analysis report must include information on the actual sales of properties in an area. These include details on the prices of properties that sold. Sometimes the property you want to acquire might be included in the report. You could get information on how much the property sold for in the past.

The actual sales report should include information based on a specific time period. It might be for a few months or a year. Sometimes the term is even longer.

Projected Sale Comparison

The actual sales section may also include details on projected sale numbers. Projections might have been made in the past based on how the properties sold in the past. This could also include how the market is doing and how good sales were and how the market grew or contraction reports that were issued.

Identifying the projected sales and how the actual sales compare is vital to understanding how a market is developing. A market might be more viable if the actual sales are greater than what the projections were. Meanwhile, a market might be too risky to get into if the actual sales are weak.

Sometimes the projections might have come about from more complicated bits of data that might not be fully accurate. These could be as a result of changes in a market or sudden events that took place in an area or within a property.

A Good Analytical Point

The comparison of actual and projected sales totals can help you identify what the market is doing. Sometimes the sales totals in an area might be higher than what people projected them to be. This is a sign that people are confident in a market. It shows that people want to buy properties in an area and are willing to invest.

If the actual sales are poor it might suggest that there is something difficult happening within a local market. This could be as a result of people moving out of an area, foreclosures, or anything else that could hurt the local region.

There is always going to be a reason why the market is overperforming or underperforming. You would have to do additional research to see what is causing the market to act in a particular way. The sales analysis report would simply be your guide toward helping you understand what is causing a market to change.

How Great Should the Difference Be?

The difference between the actual and projected sales totals should not be too great. The actual sales should be around 5 to 10 percent off the projected totals in most cases. This is enough to suggest that the market is moving normally and that projections are accurate.

How Long Should the Report Go Back?

The sales analysis report can go back as far as you want it to. It does take more effort to get historical data from several years back, but that can give you a better idea of what the long-term picture for investing in a market is like. This gives you an idea of what you can expect to find and how well the market is doing.

Knowing the past sales in the market is important to help you see what happened in the market in past years. Never assume that the projected sales are always going to react the same year after year. You must be aware that the market might change over time.

Chapter 33: Potential Income Analysis

The next point you might find on a sales analysis report is the income that you might earn off of a property. This is vital if you are looking to invest in a commercial or industrial property or even a residential site like an apartment building.

The importance of the potential income analysis is something that cannot be ignored. The tenants you engage with can make your investment.

This analysis is often included in a report to help you see what opportunity exists for a property. It also impacts the overall estimate of a property as a property with a higher potential income might be more valuable than another more attractive property. The potential income that you are anticipating from your investment can be found in the report. The analysis will at least give you an idea of what you could expect from a certain property.

What the Income Measures

The potential income analysis specifically measures the income that you would collect if the property you are investing in was completely occupied. This is also assuming that all the people in that property actually pay the rent as it is owed.

You can use this income measurement to see what you would spend on a property before you actually invest in it. This could give you more control over what you want to do in the negotiation process.

Analysis Example

The good thing about the income analysis is that it is not hard to figure out. Here is an example of how you might calculate the potential income of an investment:

1. You have ten units in an apartment building that you are buying. Eight tenants pay rent of $600 per month and two other tenants pay $1,000 per month for the larger units.

2. Add the rents: 8x600 and 2x1000.

3. 4,800 + 2,000 = 6,800. Therefore, you would receive $6,800 per month in potential income assuming the units are fully occupied and the tenants pay you on time.

Why Is It Called Potential Income?

This part of the sales analysis report indicates potential income because it involves the greatest income that you could collect. There is never a guarantee that a property will be totally occupied at all times or that the rents will actually be paid on time.

You would have to take the potential income and adjust the calculation based on any changes that might happen. You would have to consider what that total income would be if you were to remove a single unit or two.

Let's go back to the example. What if one of the $1,000 units was not occupied, or the renter did not pay the rent on time? At this point, you would have a potential income of $5,800 per month.

Now consider what might happen over time if the gap in the potential income is not resolved soon. There is a chance that the losses in the income could become significant.

The worst part of this is that it is impossible to tell when you might have gaps in your potential income. You might have a gap due to the local economy struggling or this could also happen due to a local market not being popular enough to attract more people.

The potential income you could get out of an investment might be intriguing, but there is always a chance that you might not receive that income.

Don't Forget Expenses

You can never forget the regular expenses that come with owning a property. These include property taxes, maintenance charges, utilities, renovation expenses, and cleaning costs. When you review those expenses, you should at least calculate sensible rents that will help cover or partially cover those added costs.

You will need that money not to increase your profit but to at least improving your property or covering for any emergency issues that may come about.

Success Is Up to You

In the end, the potential income is all up to you. You will learn in a later chapter about what you can do to be a better landlord so you can actually attain the potential income you want.

Chapter 34: Negotiation

So you've found a property that you want to invest in. You know that it is in a market that you feel will be worth investing in well into the future. You may also have plans for getting the value of that property to increase or to make it more appealing to possible tenants. You have the funding available to pay for the property.

In all probability your initial offer might not be attractive to the seller. You now have to consider how you will negotiate a deal with the seller. Negotiation is a vital part of the real estate investment process that you cannot afford to ignore. This is where you will talk with someone who holds a property about adjusting the terms associated with a purchase. The goal is to come up with an agreement that you and the other party will agree upon.

Negotiations often require both sides to sacrifice some of the things that they want. It is all about making a good deal. It is about ensuring that both sides are happy with the process. When both sides are satisfied, the transaction will move forward. You have to have the best possible negotiation skills to ensure you get the best possible deal.

You must also have a good strategy to begin the negotiations. To do this, you have to know what you are talking about and everything about the property, the comps, and the area.

What Will People Ask During Negotiations?

There are various factors that can directly influence what you might spend on a property and should be discussed clearly and carefully during the overall negotiation process.

Factors to be negotiated:

- Price

- Closing costs

The closing costs may include the taxes and insurance costs that have to be added to the property value. Even the service charges associated with getting the property sold can be a factor.

- The closing date

The closing date is day the purchasing funds for the property is to be sent to the lawyer. You could extend the closing date to give yourself more time to transfer the money but this might be risky.

- Plans for the financing

This is for cases where a buyer is getting financing directly from the seller's agent. Sometimes the plans might simply be just selling an old property to provide the funds needed.

- The home warranty

The negotiations might include different terms for a home warranty. A buyer can ask to have a home warranty added. A warranty should cover the utilities, appliances and other items in a property that might require repair.

- How much should the seller contribute for repairs?

A full analysis of the property and what has to be repaired should be estimated at the start of the transaction. A buyer could try and get a seller to contribute to some or all of the repairs. You can also use this part of negotiations to discuss the inspections and how dangerous materials like radon, asbestos, or lead paint will be removed if they are found.

- Furniture or appliances

A buyer might ask the seller to include the furniture, window coverings, or appliances in the sale.

- Inspection charges

The cost to get a property inspected should be decided before the offer is made and it is generally paid for by the prospective buyer. A buyer might ask the seller to cover the cost of the inspection. Sometimes a buyer might be willing to pay for the inspection and sometimes not.

Understand the Property

Negotiations can be a challenge if you come to them uninformed. You must know as much about the property as possible if you want to succeed and get the most out of any negotiation.

The first thing to do when negotiating with someone is to understand everything about the property.

Neighborhood

Look at what the local neighborhood is like and how it is laid out. You might find some interesting things relating to the property and the neighborhood that can be to your benefit. Look into the following points:

- Services and businesses in an area.

- Any common areas that might increase the value of a property.

- Roads in an area and how important they are for reaching work and amenities.

- Other properties in an area and what they might have sold for in the past.

- Future potential for a local area; this includes any new construction plans or growth rates within the region.

Having as much information on the neighborhood available as possible helps you to understand what is involved. This knowledge will do more than just help you plan the negotiation strategy you wish to use.

Physical Features of the Property

Complete as much research on a property as possible so you know what you are discussing. Try and schedule a physical visit to the property to get an even better idea of the inside and outside of the property. Having a good review of your property helps you to understand what makes a property worth investing in.

Check on as many of the physical points involving the property as you can. These include such valuable points as:

- What is the square footage of the property.

- The number of rooms in the building.

- The intentions for these rooms; these include bedrooms or bathrooms for a residential property or office spaces for a commercial site.

- Hallways, garages, basements, and other features in the property that multiple people in a property might have regular access to.

- The outside features of the property.

- The condition of the building; this includes whether the building needs to be repaired.

- Any unique amenities close to the property: pools, bars, schools, churches, library, and shopping.

- The landscape and other features around the buildings.

- Any features of the land that you would be entitled to while owning the property.

You must show evidence when you are negotiating that you know the property and the area.

Chapter 35: Making Concessions in Negotiations

It is often hard to compromise on things you want included. It is through compromise that we often get things done. One side has to give up something and vice versa.

You will have to make concessions when you are negotiating. A concession is a trade-off that you would make with the other party, in this case, the seller. When you concede to something, you are expecting something in return.

This is a vital part of negotiations to get the best deal in a real estate transaction. Even more importantly, concessions show how committed you are to something you want to acquire. You will show the other party that you are so committed that you are willing to give up something to get that property.

You must plan your concessions ahead of time so you fully understand what you could use when negotiating. You have to fully understand all that come with making concessions. You do not want to concede too much and give up more than what you can afford. You must be the one in control of the negotiations so that the other party is not going to take advantage of you.

Concessions Are Expected

You might feel as though you can get through the negotiation process without the need to make a concession. However, you will need to concede on at least one point and the other side might not be willing to make concessions if it is not necessary. Regardless of how large or small it is, you must know that your seller is not going to accept what you are offering right away. You will probably have to do some convincing.

People expect these concessions because they know they are what drive the negotiation process forward. When both sides know what they will sacrifice, they will keep the negotiations moving toward a resolution. Be ready to think about what you can do to get through the discussion by looking at what you are willing to concede.

The most important thing is that the negotiation is about cooperation, not about trying to win. The goal is to have both sides feel as though they have won. While you should aim to make the deal go in your favor, you should still be restrained and consider the needs that the other party. Do not try and be overly competitive. Instead, think about how you and the other party will feel about the transaction.

This is not a one-sided affair in the least. Treating it that way would only cause a significant impasse in the discussions you are trying to hold. Besides, you should give the seller a feeling of satisfaction when the transaction is completed.

Decide onYour Concessions

There are many steps you can use when deciding what you are willing to concede. To give yourself more support for planning your negotiations:

1. Prepare a list of things that are important to you.

2. Organize those things based on whether they are very important or if you are willing to sacrifice them.

Plan a list in order from what is more important to what is least important.

3. Give some thought about what the seller might feel about what you consider to be most important.

The seller might place a certain value on what you are willing to give up.

4. Prepare the terms you are using in words that the other party will understand.

Avoid using complicated language. You don't need to use legalese to make your point. Use plain and easy-to-understand language that cannot be misinterpreted.

5. Decide how many concessions you are willing to make.

Have a smart plan to have a good chance of getting what you want.

What Will You Concede?

You could concede practically anything associated with the property. You could say you are willing to cover the cost of any repairs that a property needs, for instance. Maybe you might offer to manage all the insurance policies on the property yourself. Whatever the case, you have to show that will not be too demanding in the negotiation.

You should only offer concessions if you are able to afford them.

What Will You Get in Return?

When you create your list of concessions, you will notice that each item holds some value. Think carefully about what you can get in return for each concession you make.

You must never make any concessions unless you can get something in return. That return must be equal in value to your concession.

As you plan your concessions, you must establish them in a way that the other party knows what you will concede and what its value to you is. This lets the other party know that your concession is made so that you are assured to get something of equal value in return.

When Should You Make the Concessions?

Whatever you do, avoid making the concessions too early. Making concessions really early in the process is a sign of weakness. It suggests that you are willing to accept just about anything he wants to give you.

Any concessions that come about too early might not seem genuine. You need to give your negotiating partner the ideas that you are willing to fight and get what you want. That other person will appreciate you when you are trying to get more out of a contract. It shows how serious you are about the investment you want to enter into.

Can You Withdraw a Concession?

Do not assume that the concessions you wish to make are final after they are introduced or agreed upon. The negotiation process can be extremely complicated. It might go through several changes.

The seller must assume that any concessions you are offering are temporary. The seller has to put in enough effort to make those concessions final. You have the option to remove those conditions if you feel the seller is not giving you a fair deal.

Is Splitting the Difference a Good Idea?

It is true that you could find a middle point between your offer and the seller's bottom line.

A middle point illustrates a compromise of sorts. You could use the concessions to make it easier for you and the seller to get to that middle point. You just have to review the specific concessions you want to use and then figure out how they are to be placed to get you as close to the middle as possible. Is that always going to be the best move?

One strategy to using concessions is to split the difference. It is an interesting move that in theory allows for concessions on both sides. Splitting the difference is a process where you take the two proposals and take in the average of the two. For instance, you might get a home you want to invest in at $170,000 while the seller wants $180,000. You might try to split the difference and get the property for $175,000.

That sounds like a great move, right? After all, everyone loves a good compromise. This is not necessarily going to work as well as you might think. If anything, you could actually do better than this.

At this point, you are actually shifting the negotiating upward. You have gone from negotiation at a range of $170k-180k to $175k-180k. In other words, you are not only going to pay more than what you had hoped, but there is a chance that the cost is only going to get higher.

Eventually, the seller will try to split the difference again and offer a deal of $177,500 for the property. This is much more than what the original offer was.

The truth is that splitting the difference is not necessarily going to be the right thing to do for the transaction. In most cases, it is the seller that will try to get you to pay more for the property. The seller could play hardball and you concede and then split the difference yourself. This only makes it harder for you to get a better deal on the property. The fact that a party could split the difference multiple times in the transaction only makes things worse.

The most important part of splitting the difference is to never make this suggestion yourself. Let the seller suggest splitting the difference. When you do this, you will suggest to the seller that you are willing to compromise. At this point, you could agree to the proposal if it is good for you. The seller will feel as though he won, but you will benefit the most because you will have lowered the total price.

Keep Track of Concessions

The negotiation process can be extremely complicated. You could lose track of some of the concessions you are willing to make. You might miss one thing that a person is willing to offer. This could end up by conceded too many things.

Keep tabs on what you and the other party have done. Feel free to build upon what other side is doing and that you know what is moving forward and changing within the negotiation.

Trust Is Vital

Regardless of what the concessions might be, you must present them in a way that is fair to the other party. You must let the other person know that you care about his needs and you want to handle the transaction fairly. Your concessions will become more credible when you show that you are interested in the well-being of the other party. More importantly, those concessions will be easier for the other person to accept.

You can also gain the trust of the other party by avoiding the emotional appeals that come with concessions. Showing too much emotion, in this case, is a sign of weakness. It suggests that you are not ready for a transaction.

Compare Other Properties

The most important point of concessions is to look at all the other properties you might find in the local area. You have many options to choose from when investing. You can always let the seller know that you are willing to make an offer on another property if this one does not work out. To make this plan work, you would have to understand what comparables are in your area and their value.

Having an idea of what the values of comparables gives you ammunition to negotiate. You would have to mention properties that are true comparables keep the value reasonable.

The seller will notice that you have a clear idea of what the market is like and that a property might be worth. This knowledge will be to your benefit and help you get a property that you want.

Concessions are a vital part of negotiations for you to be successful.

Chapter 36: Negotiation Strategies

Negotiations can take some time to complete. You might spend weeks or even months trying to get a deal set up with someone. This is a process that requires lots of effort on your. Prepare a sensible plan for getting the terms that you want.

A negotiation strategy is a process where you will attempt to adjust the offers that you put to a seller. You can choose to add or remove anything you want into or out of the offer during the negotiation process. The goal is to create a good deal that works in your favor.

The negotiations should help you manage both the needs you have and what the other party is looking for. In other words, your strategy should leave something for the other person to appreciate and support. However, it is all about not only making it easier for a deal to be accepted but also to help get more of what you want out of the deal.

Nibbling

Nibbling is a strategy where you make the seller feel as though the property you are looking into is cheap.

Nibbling gets its name from how you eat away at the overall value here and there. This helps you to get the demands you want while keeping yourself from spending too much for the property.

This is how this strategy works:

1. You've found a property worth $400,000 that you want to buy. Try and let the seller know about things that you need to add to the property and what you feel might be necessary for repairs.

2. Ask about what it might cost to get something new added to a property. This could include a new roof or new flooring.

3. Keep making as many requests as possible. After a while, the seller should be more likely to sell you the property for less.

This is a good move, but some sellers might feel that you are taking them for a ride. A seller might say that you are too demanding. In other cases, the seller might think that a demand you have is unrealistic and that something you want to do with a property is not necessary. That person might think a property does not need a new roof. Be cautious when nibbling and be aware of how the seller responds.

Hot Potato

The next strategy to use is the hot potato strategy. This is a move that helps you to explain some kind of difficulty you have. The strategy helps you to reduce the price that you are willing to spend on the property.

The key is that you are introducing something that might keep you from buying the property. The seller will have to find a way to reduce the price so that he persuades you to buy the property.

Here is a look at what can happen with the hot potato strategy:

1. You might need to spend $250,000 on the property. Maybe you do not have the money for a down payment worth 20 percent of that total.

2. You can explain some kind of personal issue or financing issue you have that is keeping the deal from moving forward.

3. Ask the seller to adjust the value to make it easier for you to afford the property. The seller should be willing to make a few changes to the price at this point.

You must be logical and realistic when trying to use the hot potato strategy. Refer to things that are actually happening in your life if possible.

Be aware that some sellers might be suspicious of the things you are saying. A seller might try and talk you through some of the problems you have. That person could ask for proof relating to an issue or even think about what can happen a few weeks or months from now. The hot potato strategy works only when you know you have a plan for proving the problems you have. This is a high-risk solution for negotiating, but it could be worthwhile if you are careful.

Good vs. Bad Guy

This third negotiation strategy is one where you are the good guy while the seller is the bad guy. This requires you to be adamant on certain demands or interests that you have. You are illustrating your offer as a good one while the seller does not have the same values in mind.

Here is how this strategy works:

1. You are looking to buy a home for $300,000. You might have a list of demands for the seller.

2. Present the demands and illustrate that you feel the deal is ready to be made. Show that you are committed.

3. The seller will deny the offer and any demands that you put forward.

4. You would counter the offer with the same points or even with one or two alterations. The goal is to keep the

value of the property around the same value of $300,000.

The main goal is to convince the seller to move the transaction forward. The seller should be willing to listen to you and hear you out. Be advised that some sellers are not always willing to budge. They might feel you are too confrontational or otherwise hard to deal with.

Desperation

The desperation strategy has a slightly misleading title. It is not about you sounding desperate. Rather, it is about knowing when the seller is desperate and really wants to get a property off his hands. This is about taking advantage of when someone really wants to sell a property and is anxious to do so.

You can use the desperation strategy to target a home seller that wants to hurry with a sale. Sometimes a seller might want to get rid of a home because it is distressed and needs many repairs. In other cases, that person might be trying to get it sold fast due to a pending foreclosure or even a correction or other significant change in the market.

You can use some steps to take advantage of someone's desperation:

1. Complete as much research on the property as possible. Look into the market as well.

2. Ask questions about why the seller wants to sell the property.

3. Address issues relating to repairs, foreclosures or other problems with the property.

4. Decrease the value of the property at this point. By linking your cuts to the points that are causing the

seller to be desperate, it becomes easier for you to get the property that you want.

Identifying someone's desperation and worry about a property is vital to getting more out of your investment. You must see if a seller is struggling and address those problems. The seller will be relieved to have sold property at this point. More importantly, you will have made a great.

Illustrate Empathy

One negotiating strategy that sounds simple but goes far is showing a sense of empathy toward the seller. Empathy shows you know what your seller wants and that you understand that person's needs. Illustrating that you know what the seller is thinking and that you are placing yourself in that person's shoes is always worth doing.

Empathy makes it easier for a seller to appreciate you. That seller might give you some of the demands you have made or reduce the cost of the property.

Here are a few things you can do to show empathy:

1. Write a letter to the seller during the transaction process. Explain in your letter that you have a strong desire for the home and that you feel it is right for your needs. You can talk about your personal needs for a property at this point.

2. Visit the seller's office if you can. Having a one-on-one meeting helps you to understand the needs that the seller has while expressing your concerns and desires.

3. Talk with the seller about his work and what he might have done in the past.

Showing empathy can go a long way toward getting a better deal on a property. You can show empathy to illustrate that you understand the situation of the seller. Be calm and gracious.

Do not probe into the seller's life or personal situation. The best form of empathy always comes naturally. You have to let the seller know that you care and that you are willing to make a good deal with that person. Offer a generic statement of support without going into detail.

Negotiations can be worthwhile for helping you to get what you want out of your real estate investment plans. Consider the strategy you plan on using and that you have a good idea for how it will work.

Chapter 37: Planning a Favorable and Profitable Contract

After you negotiate a plan for a real estate investment, you can get a contract set up. This is the overall agreement that you will use for accepting and paying for the property. It lists the rules surrounding your investment and how you are going to make it work. The terms associated with the contract can be complex, but it is something that has to be planned accordingly for the best possible results.

You must establish a suitable contract. A great contract will have not only the terms but also the rules to be followed in the event anything difficult might come about during the transfer of funds and registering the property in your name.

A quick note: Some of the points listed here relate to simply buying the property. A few terms here involve what happens when you plan on selling a property you already have to buy a new one. The circumstances of your situation may vary.

A Bilateral Deal

The contract that you set up must be bilateral. This means that the seller agrees to sell a property while the buyer agrees to buy it. This is a simple meaning, but it is one that makes a real difference when the contract is being written. Both sides have to agree.

This is a fair and useful contract that is appropriate for any transaction you wish to make. With a bilateral deal, one person makes a promise to conduct a certain action in response to the action of the other party. It is a peaceful and simple approach to getting a transaction handled that should be easy to organize without being complicated.

Avoid Unilateral Deals

A unilateral deal is one where one person can make an agreement. For a real estate investment, the buyer could agree to buy the property while the seller could still refuse to sell. The seller at this juncture is not obligated to sell the property.

The big difference between a unilateral and bilateral contract is that a bilateral contract is something that can be enforced right away. Both parties in the bilateral agreement are bound to the terms of the contract. A unilateral deal has just one party promising to pay when certain terms are met.

This does not mean you cannot add particular terms to a contract. As you will see in the next chapter, you can always use a few contingencies when buying a property, but those would have to be added before the bilateral agreement is made.

Purchase Price Setup

The purchase price for the property should be as specific as possible. The price must only be listed after an appraisal has been done on the property. The price should be solidified at this point to ensure that both the buyer and seller have a clear idea of what the property is worth.

The price should have been properly figured out based on the appraisal of a property or other reviews. The price might have been determined based on the negotiations that were held as well.

Identified Parties

The two parties taking part in the transaction must be clearly identified. One problem that comes with many contracts is that they are not explicit so that people know who is buying a property or who is selling it. A clear definition must be made to ensure the data in the transaction is correct. You can include information in the contract about who will buy the property and who is responsible after the transaction goes through.

The names of individuals should be listed. If a trust or other larger group is involved, the names of the people who are in charge of the trust should be included. List all the names of owners and sellers of the property in the agreement to avoid any confusion.

Break Clause

A break clause can be added to the contract if necessary. This is a clause stating that a contract, lease, or other agreement can be broken early if necessary. This means that the agreement for buying a home could be broken. Break clauses work for home purchases, but they can also work for leasing out areas in a commercial or industrial site.

There are many reasons why a contract might have to be broken:

- The funds needed for getting a home sold might not be available.

- A buyer is not paying the loans attached to the contract.

- Some issues might come about surrounding the home that might make it difficult for the home to be useful. This could keep the existing agreement from being suitable or reasonable.

- The closure of a property that you are investing in can force you to break a contract.

Adding a break clause ensures you can get out of the contract without any penalties. Some sellers like to add penalties to their break clauses. These should be written out before you agree to anything. Rules on when the fees associated with a break clause can be applied should be added too. Sometimes you might not have to pay anything for such a clause due to the circumstances surrounding the issue being outside of your control.

Length of Lease

The length of a lease should be reviewed and understood. This is when you are investing in a few units in an apartment building or office space. You could place an agreement stating that you will pay a set amount of money per month on specific units over an extended time.

The lease length might be for a full year in most cases. Sometimes you might get a longer lease in exchange for cheaper monthly payments. Every seller has their own rules for what it set as your lease payments.

Length of Sale Agreement

Perhaps you are aiming to sell a property before you can buy the property you are dealing with. When this happens, you can choose to establish a point in your contract that refers to the length of the agreement. This includes information about how long the seller will wait before completing the sale of your old property.

The length of the agreement refers to how long it will take for the buyer to work toward selling off his property. This is a conditional sale and the length of the conditional sale could be a few months for an entire year. The average length of an agreement is for about six months. Meanwhile, a commission of 1 or 2 percent of the value of the property after it is sold may be charged to the buyer, but this charge is also flexible and can be agreed to or not.

Protection Clause

A protection clause may be added that would include protection from having to pay someone a commission in the event the listing for your old property expires. A protection clause may last for about 30 to 90 days after the original contract expired. You should use this to protect yourself in the event you have any problems surrounding the sale of your property.

Exclusion Clause

An exclusion clause allows the seller to sell his property to someone else if another offer is presented from a buyer #2 during the time buyer #1 has been given to sell his property to buy the seller's property. It gives the seller the opportunity to sell his property and not wait for months or a year to complete the sale. It puts the buyer #1 on notice that they have a certain length of time (usually 24-48 hours) to firm up the deal or to walk away.

Description of the Property

A specific description of a property should be included in the contract. This does more than just tell people what the contract is for. It also includes details on everything that is being covered and included in the contract.

The description has to include as many features as possible:

- The property's physical address and legal description.

- The physical features of the property.

- The types and number of rooms.

- The description of a garage, and/or out buildings on the property.

- Any landscaping features or other identifying points.

- Any and all items that are included in the sale – window coverings, appliances etc.

It reveals that you bought the investment based on certain physical conditions. The description should be as detailed or specific as possible.

Chapter 38: Contingencies of a Contract

Contingencies are important to apply to the transaction before a contract is established. These are rules for when certain conditions are met.

A contingency works with a few steps:

1. You will establish a contingency in your contract.

2. The seller will have to meet the terms associated with the contingency.

3. Another event relating to the contingency may also be met depending on its terms.

4. After each contingency in a contract is passed, you can officially acquire a property.

There are no guarantees that you will have to go through any of these contingencies, but it still helps to add them to your purchase document to be safe. You never know when you might run into a situation where one of these contingencies has to be triggered.

A contingency might be used to allow you to discontinue a contract in the event any issues come about within a home. These include problems relating to a home's construction or any features failing in the property.

You must be specific for when certain conditions can be met. Your goal is to establish a plan where people will be confident in what is being offered and that you know how the contract will be honored.

Appraisal

You can ask for an appraisal contingency where a property will be purchased upon receiving the proper appraisal. When you get a loan, you might be told by the lender to get an appraisal on the property. Your contingency for an appraisal could be based on how much money the property is worth. This includes the total value that is determined based on the appraisal. You will have the option to retract your offer if the property is within a certain range outside of what you want to spend.

Inspection

An inspection contingency can cover points relating to a property regarding structural issues, lead paint, asbestos, inadequate wiring, plumbing, or roofing materials, and other harmful concerns. A contingency may be placed stating that you will only agree to a purchase the property if the problems that are found during the inspection are resolved. You could ask the seller to pay for the repairs.

Roof Inspection

Not all inspections include the roof. You can include a roof inspection and repairs in a contingency. Demand that a certified inspector is used because a roofing company might try and take advantage and suggest that a roof needs repairs or replacing when it is not necessary. A professional inspector will provide a fair and neutral assessment of the roof without being pressured by one side or the other.

Sewer Inspection

Sewer inspections are not often conducted by real estate sellers either. A sewer inspection can help you identify problems relating to the sewer line. A camera might be used by an inspector to identify issues relating to clogs, dislodged pipes, and other problems. You must add a contingency clause stating that the sewer line must be inspected and fixed before you will continue with the purchase.

Selling an Existing Home

Are you trying to sell one real estate investment to get into a different one? It may also be a challenge to manage if you are unable to get that older property sold.

It is strongly recommended in this situation that you buy the new investment first and then sell the old one. When you do this, you have to include a contingency stating that the contract for a property is dependent on your ability to sell you other property. You can state in the purchase contract that you will be given a certain number of days to sell the old property in order to complete the purchase of the new one.

Doing this ensures that you will get the new property you want even before the property you already have is sold. This could make it easier for the seller to accept a deal too. The seller will know that the money from the sale of your property is committed to the new purchase.

An Important Note

Adding contingencies to your transaction does not mean you are entering into a unilateral contract. With contingencies, you will explain that a bilateral contract can be set up and agreed upon after certain things are done to a property. The goal is to keep the transaction fair and suitable for everyone without any surprises happening.

Chapter 39: Working With a Real Estate Investment Trust

Much of what you have been reading thus far about investing in real estate has been about buying a property on your own. You don't have to go it alone. You can work with a real estate trust to acquire an investment property.

Specifically, you can work with a real estate investment trust to find a property. Also known as a REIT, this trust helps you to invest in a real estate property without having to actually buy a physical property. It is an intriguing option for investment, but it does have some issues you must understand.

This option makes the real estate investing field accessible and attractive. It gives you an opportunity to move into the field without having to purchase an entire property. When you consider being involved with a REIT, you will have to review the market and determine the advantages for you. This is a potentially profitable option, but it is always at risk of losing value just like with anything else involving property.

What Is A REIT?

A REIT is a trust that has been legal in the United States since it was first introduced through an act of Congress in 1960. It allows people to invest in real estate even if they do not have a lot of money or access to a loan.

The best way to describe a REIT is that it works as an exchanged-traded fund. It holds many types of real estate and may pay off based on how it performs on the overall market. Here is an explanation of how a REIT works:

1. An investor will buy shares of a particular REIT.

2. The investor will review how the REIT is performing in the market.

3. The value of the REIT will change based on how the values of properties associated with the trust change. The change in value will vary.

4. Dividend distributions will be sent out to the investor. These returns are sized based on the actual amount of money someone has invested.

What Does A REIT Include?

There are no real rules for what a REIT absolutely has to include, but a REIT will need to incorporate various properties. The trust will be run by a larger equity firm that operates within the real estate investment firm. You can talk with a financial broker to learn more about the many parties that are trading REITs on the market. These include Vanguard, Charles Schwab, SPDR, and iShares among others.

A REIT will feature assets operated by real estate service providers. These include assets held by groups that buy and sell properties and rent them to people:

- Most REITs focus heavily on residential and commercial properties.

- Some REITs work with specific types of property investments. These include resorts, hospitality sites, healthcare sites, and even shopping malls.

- Others may include small investments for timber and other raw materials needed for building new real estate assets. Less than 5 percent of a typical REIT will include funds for those types of investments.

What to Find In a REIT

You must be careful when looking for a REIT as the choices are vast.

Here are a few points to review when looking into a REIT:

- Review the company that is offering the REIT.

The financial services broker or other investment team offering the REIT should be experienced and offer enough support for your investment. It should be ready to answer any questions you have while providing research for any trust you wish to enter.

- Review the assets of the trust. Look at how diverse or focused the assets are in one particular segment of real estate.

- Check the total value of the net assets in the trust.

- Review the yield and the YTD return on the trust.

Be advised that while a good yield suggests that a trust might be profitable, there is no real way you can be assured you will actually gain the yield. If anything, the trust is always at risk of losing money.

- Look into the history of the trust. The firm offering the trust to you should be open with information on what the trust has done in the past.

- Look how the dividend payment ratios are established. This determines if you can expect dividends and how much.

- Find and read any outside reviews relating to the REIT you are considering.

Sometimes outside reviews will provide you with extra information on how well a REIT is performing, how it pays dividends, and even how the people who provide the REIT might share information on it.

The best way to review a REIT is to look into it like you would any other stock purchase, mutual fund, or other investment. The REIT is designed to focus on real estate but not necessarily foreign in nature. Checking on how a trust performs over time and analyzing the full report surrounding what it includes always helps you to decide what you might realize and if it will be worthwhile.

How to Get Into a REIT

After deciding the REIT you want to invest in, you can contact someone to help you with the process. There are a few steps:

1. Contact an investment broker about a REIT you wish to join.

2. Review all the terms associated with the REIT. These include any fees involved and how the trust might change over time.

3. Talk with the broker about how well the REIT is performing and what you can expect as a return. The broker should explain everything about it and how it can work for your investment plans.

4. Determine the total amount of money you wish to add to the REIT.

5. You should officially be included in the REIT after depositing your funds into the trust.

This is a simple process that does not involve much for you to do. Entering a REIT can be rewarding and could be worthwhile if you do not have the money needed for investing in real estate in a more traditional manner.

You will have to confirm your identity and transfer money into the trust. You may also need to meet with an advisor who can give you full information on the risks and other features of the trust.

Pros of a REIT

The thrill of moving into a REIT is something that more people have been looking into than ever before. They are excited about how a REIT works and what it can offer. There are many good reasons why entering a REIT is a good idea to consider for real estate investing:

- Yields can be strong depending on what you invest in.

- The REIT must pay a certain amount of money to its investors in the form of dividends.

A REIT typically needs to spend 90 percent of its income to its members. The broker or firm that runs the trust can use a higher total if desired, but that firm cannot go any lower than 90 percent in most instances.

- Your REIT makes it easier for you to enter into the real estate investment field.

- The diverse array of properties in the REIT makes it a useful option.

- You can sell your shares when you wish to cash out of the trust. This is much easier to do than selling an actual real estate property.

- The costs associated with a REIT vary based on who you contact but are still less than what you would pay to purchase a traditional property.

The costs associated with a REIT might have charges apply for keeping the trust maintained or for making trades, but these costs are less than whatever you might spend on a regular real estate property.

Cons of a REIT

As attractive as a REIT might be, you would have to be aware of problems that come with a REIT. The following are some of the cons:

- There is always a chance that the value of the trust may decline.

You are not immune from cases where property values can decline while in a REIT. The properties in the trust can weaken in value based on the real estate market's performance. Even vacancies in properties that are included in the trust could weaken its value by the potential for rent payments to be substantially lower than usual.

- The demand for a trust might be influenced by how the stock market is changing. The trust value might change if the market is shrinking.

- A REIT might try to expand its holdings to manage the dividends.

This aspect of a REIT is risky in that the trust will have to do what it can to increase the various investments it has. The trust might need to incur a debt to expand what it owns due to the dividends being so high.

- Many REITs are taxable.

You might be taxed 15 percent of the profits you receive from the REIT.

Overall, a REIT is an attractive option to look into when finding a way to invest in real estate. You can use this kind of trust to get money without having to contend with the financial burden you would have in purchasing and maintaining a real property.

Chapter 40: How to Increase the Value of a Property

The biggest point about investing in real estate involves getting the value of your property to go up in value. You need to increase the value of your property so you can get the most out of your investment. This is especially critical when you see how much money you are spending to acquire a property in the first place. There are many options to choose from increasing the value of your property.

This chapter is about some of the things you can do to help make your property more valuable and attractive to potential investors. These ideas work well regardless of the property you are investing in.

Repair Your Property

The first and most basic thing to do to increase the value of an investment is to complete as many repairs as possible. It is easier for the property to increase when it is in good repair and works even better when you wish to flip a house.

How much of an impact will home repairs have on the value of your property? The total will vary based on what you do. You can expect the value of a property to increase from 10 to 30 percent after the appropriate repairs are completed. You can always research other properties in an area to see what their values might have changed after repairs were done so you have an idea of what you could spend in the process.

Remove Anything Dangerous

Always get rid of any asbestos, radon, lead paint, lead pipes, and other risky items out of your property if possible. You should have received a full inspection of your property before you bought it. There is always that potential that something might come about that was not found in the initial inspection.

For instance, radon might appear in your home even after you found earlier that it was nowhere to be found. The earth shifts naturally and your foundation might deteriorate after a while, thus allowing radon to enter. You would have to get it taken care of soon so the problem can be resolved.

Removing dangerous items is important to do because those compounds could keep the value of your home from being as high as it should. Even worse, a person who wants to buy your property might refuse to make an offer if asbestos or lead among other dangerous things were found. Get your property tested to ensure it is safe and not a threat. This will surely increase your investment value.

Add More Room

You can add some extra room to your property. Adding extra space not only adds to the square footage of a property but also makes it more functional. You might be able to add new bedrooms or bathrooms into a home or maybe a few new office spaces for individual tenants.

You can also add more room by building a new structure on the plot of land you own. Whether it is a guest house, a small office, a garage, or even a barn building for a property on an agricultural or ranch zoning area, you could always use a the new build to add extra value for your property.

Adding extra room often requires lots of money. The cost to add an extension to a property could be high. You would have to keep that extension consistent with the rest of the existing property too.

Permits would have to be applied for. Depending on your location, you might not be allowed to build what you want. This might be frustrating, but it is a point that deserves to be noticed because you have to conform to the zoning and building rules regardless of what area your property is situated.

Establish a Better Sense of Curb Appeal

The potential for you to have a better return on your investment will be strong when you establish a great outside look to your home. Having a good curb appeal is important as it makes people want to come to your home or inside your home. A person might be confident in a property when it has a strong sense of curb appeal. This could improve the value of your property.

The solutions you can use for improving your curb appeal include:

- Review the paint job on the property. It might need a lighter color or repainting.

- Maintain the lawn and replace any old or dying area with a new sod. Keep the lawn consistent in its appearance too.

- Any trees in an area should be trimmed to keep them from overpowering an area or interfere with utilities.

- Add a deck or patio in the front if you do not have one.

Keep this part consistent with the look of other homes in an area. The patio or deck should also blend with the rest of the outside of the home.

- Add or repair walkways.

- Shrubs, plants and other greenery can be added to the landscaping provided they do not obstruct windows or other critical features of your home.

- Construct a fence that is in keeping with other properties on your street.

Common Mistakes When Repairing or Renovating

While repairing or renovating a home can increase its value, there is always the chance that a property value might not actually increase because might be doing something the wrong way. Maybe you are adding something that you really do not need. Whatever the case, you could be doing something that would actually hurt your property more than it would actually help it.

There are various mistakes you should avoid when trying to fix a home to improve its value:

- Avoid being trendy when creating a new layout or look.

A trendy modern look might not be as valuable a few years from now as it is today. You could always work with classic designs and layouts for your property to ensure it has a steady value well into the future.

- Keep any improvements you make looking as great and unique as possible.

You do not want to make any questionable improvements that might not look all that attractive. Your property could lose value if you have crooked tiles, visible nails, and other features that clearly show you did something with a property but did it poorly. Hiring a professional to help you fix your property is always a good option to consider so you can keep your property from looking unprofessional.

- Avoid dark colors.

Neutral or light colors are more appealing to potential buyers. They want to buy properties that look interesting and are inviting places to live in or to rent.

- Stay consistent and avoid using multiple styles.

Sometimes one room or area might overwhelm everything else in the property because it looks unusual or does not blend in well. You must allow the design and layout of your home to be consistent with each room blending in with one another. This adds a nice design that should keep or increase the value of a property.

- Don't let your property have outstanding and unusual features. An above-ground pool might sound like something fun to have, but it would make your property unattractive. The pool could look unsightly to some. Avoid using anything like this that might cause a property to be too unusual in its appearance when compared with others in the area.

Convert Individual Spaces In a Property

You can convert certain places on your property to be used for different functions. An old garage can be converted into a new bedroom, for instance.

Be advised that you would need enough construction materials on hand to finish a project. Nothing looks worse that an uncompleted project. Hire a professional if need be.

You could convert a property to accommodate a completely different intention. You could change an old office building that housed many cubicles and conference rooms into a warehouse. This could be interesting if the property is in an area where converting would be a worthwhile and profitable. The cost to make a major conversion or renovation might be very expensive. As well, you will have to apply for permits and you might have to get your property rezoned or at least ask for an exception or other permission to let you use a property for a specific intention.

Reduce Operating Costs

Properties are worth more if the cost to operate is low. People want to focus on enjoying the things in their homes, not on struggling to try and pay the utility bills. You can do many things to reduce the operating costs on a property:

- Inspect the plumbing fixtures to see how water is being used and how much. This includes fixing leaks, improving upon how water is heated and even insulating a boiler.

- Check on the insulation in a property. Replacing insulation might help to keep the conditions inside a property comfortable.

- Renewable energy materials can be added onto a property. Solar power panels are among the most popular renewable energy items. These can keep a property from using a regular energy grid.

- Replace the light fixtures with LED bulbs.

LED bulbs are popular for not only using less energy but also for lasting longer. This could help with saving money on operating costs and will be more than worth the added cost of the new LED bulbs.

Chapter 41: Gentrification

We have heard plenty of stories over the years about gentrification and how it can impact communities. We hear jokes about people who move to gentrified neighborhoods. The truth is that gentrification might actually be a good thing for real estate investments.

Gentrification is all about an area becoming more visible, attractive, and popular thanks to it feeling and looking more modern or unique. It may also be a safer place to live in. While gentrification is attractive it also has a few problems and criticisms that deserve to be explored.

What Is Gentrification?

Gentrification is a situation where properties are renovated or restored as younger or more affluent residents come into an area. This is noticeable around urban regions for the most part. People who might be wealthier will replace people who are poorer or unable to maintain their properties. Those wealthier people will help the community with renovations and being lively.

Gentrification is a concept that has been prevalent since the early Common Era. It was first noticed in the 3rd Century when many villas in Rome and parts of Britain were replacing smaller shops. People in the middle classes started to take over areas that had been inhabited by lower classes.

Gentrification is often caused by many things:

- Wealthy people are moving into an area.

This might happen because people are finding new job opportunities in an area or maybe people just looking for cheap properties that they can improve. Whatever the case, gentrification can quickly develop when the disposable income of a group of people has increased.

- Rental markets might be tight.

People who want to rent properties might struggle to find them in some areas. They might find good properties in some poorer regions. When wealthier people rent properties in these areas, they start to renovate and restore properties. This makes those areas a little more valuable.

- Some argue that bank rules might influence gentrification.

There are arguments that gentrification is caused mainly by communities recovering following bank rules that might become a serious problem in some areas. Many poor areas are inhabited by people who might have been refused bank loans for various reasons. Those who are too poor might move into certain regions that are not properly kept while the people who can afford to renovate and repair buildings will move into their old properties.

It could be a place that people are flocking to because they don't have anywhere else to go. It could also be that people simply want to find a new place that offers a change of pace and might be a little more affordable to buy.

Where Does Gentrification Take Place?

Gentrification takes place in urban areas most often. These include places that might be densely populated and have a mix of residential and commercial properties. You are not likely to see gentrified suburban areas because those areas are more removed from the center of commerce. With gentrification, an entire community will develop and evolve.

A gentrified area can be any size. Some gentrified areas might take in a few blocks. In some cases, an entire town or city could become gentrified if enough people move into that area while the old generation moves out.

Who Are These Gentrifying People?

You could find any type of person in a newly gentrified community. These include not only younger professionals and millennials, but also older seniors who might be finding appealing places to live in as they retire.

There are also now rules for how large families can be in these areas. Some gentrified areas might have families, but single and two-person units will be more prevalent. This is especially true of places where multiple apartment complexes are found. There are no rules regarding how affluent a person is to live in a community like this, nor are there any racial or cultural biases. In other words, practically anyone could be a part of a gentrified neighborhood.

Of course, fair housing laws ensure that everyone has a chance to get into a gentrified community. It does not matter what a person's background might be. All the person needs to enter into a local area is the money to buy a property and to pay it off regularly. The financial consideration is more important than anything else.

Common Signs of Gentrification

There are many signs of gentrification that you can see. Not all of these signs are prevalent in all gentrified communities, but they are good things to look for when finding such places:

- You might notice lots of construction in an area. This includes construction of new walkways or storefronts. You might notice lots of sidewalk closures or detours.

- Old businesses are being replaced with newer ones. These include not only local ones but also some national chains.

- People don't have a need for traditional vehicles. People might walk or ride bicycles more often.

- Retailers are more diverse and in some cases specific in nature. These include organic grocery stores instead of regular supermarkets or drugstores.

- Public transportation services are readily accessible. These include bus and rail services.

- There is adequate police protection and the police are willing to address noise complaints.

- The properties are well-painted and maintained. You might also see organized forms of urban art rather than random graffiti.

- Sometimes the introduction of new apartment buildings or other properties might be a big factor. These include properties that will be built on lots that used to have single-family homes.

These signs might suggest that property values will start to rise. As an area becomes gentrified and more appealing, it becomes a place that people will want to live in. This, in turn, increases the values of properties.

You can always check on reports of gentrification in an area to see how it is progressing. You can look for details on how properties are being renovated, how much money people are spending on those properties, and how businesses are changing. You might find that property values are going up thanks to how great a community is becoming and what is making the area thrive and be vibrant.

Concerns Relating to Gentrification

Although gentrification might be great for when you want to find real estate that could increase in value, there are a few problems that deserve to be considered, such as:

- Older businesses and residents might be forced out of an area. These include people who are unable to pay the more expensive rents.

- Some gentrified communities might not be diverse. They might focus on just one particular group of people or a sole demographic. This is in spite of such properties being open to everyone.

- The job markets in some gentrified areas are not always stable. Businesses could be at risk of opening and closing quickly.

- People might try to avoid some neighborhoods because they don't feel like they are lively or appealing.

- The turnover rate in a neighborhood might be high. A person could choose to live in one of these areas for just a few years. This could be a problem for people trying to invest in properties in communities where they depend on rentals.

Gentrification is an interesting thing to look into when finding properties to invest in. You have the potential to get a good deal on a property in an urban area that is growing and thriving.

Chapter 42: Being a Better Landlord

You have the option to rent out homes, condos, or office spaces in a property you own. No matter what you have to rent, you will have to try to be a great landlord. You will keep your tenants if you care for them and are reasonable to deal with.

This chapter is about what you can do to keep clients in your property and to get the right ones that will help you get the income you need from your investment.

Verify All Clients

The first thing you need to do is to verify everyone who is applying to rent from you. You need to verify people to ensure that they are safe and reliable. They should be people who will not be likely to damage your property or be a nuisance to others. You must avoid renting to people who might potentially engage in illegal activities inside your property. You need to choose renters that you can trust.

You will need to complete a background check on anyone who wants to use your property. There are a few steps you can use to do a background check:

1. Start by having a direct interview with the person who is applying to rent your property.

Meet with the person face-to-face if possible. An online visitation may work as well, but you should try to be direct with whomever you are interviewing. You can ask questions to that person relating to:

- When does the person need to begin to rent the property?

- What is their employment and are they employed?

- What is the person's existing housing situation and why does that person want to move into your property?

- Check the prospective tenant's credit report.

- Ask for at least two references from people who have rented to them before.

- The budget that tenant has.

- The living needs that person requires.

- The names of all other persons who will be living with that renter.

- Do they have pets? Does that follow your rules for pets on your property?

Getting enough information helps you to see what has inspired a person to want to rent your property. This could also help you to see if that person can afford to rent from you.

2. Start a pleasant conversation with a potential tenant.

You can learn more about a tenant by just talking with that person. Having a brief and simple conversation will help you to learn more about that person's need for a property and why they want to rent from you.

3. Review a person's identity online.

You can look for information on a tenant online after you speak with that person. There are various websites that can help you to find information on tenants like RentPrep, SmartMove, Cozy, Buildium, Screening Works, or MyRental among others. These can help you find information on people based on:

- Social Security Number validation.

- United States criminal reports.

- Sex offender details.

- Any FICO score issues or concerns one has.

- Address history.

All of these details will help you to find a good person who will be a good tenant. There is a cost involved for you to use the services of these online companies. That cost should be worthwhile when you consider the risks of not vetting a tenant properly.

4. Verify a person's income.

A tenant needs to be capable of paying the rent on a regular basis. You will have to verify a tenant's income to ensure that person can pay the rent on time.

Use one of the tenant check services listed to get information on the prospective renter's credit rating. That person should have a minimal income to debt ratio; this means the person is making more income than what they owe. The measurement could suggest that a person will continue to pay the rent to you even if a sudden debt or other issue happens.

You should also contact a candidate's employer to get information on one's employment status and how much money that person earns in a typical month. Look for copies of the last few pay stubs someone might have earned too. This information will help you get an idea of what a person might get and how consistently that person is paid. The best tenant is one that earns around three times the rent cost each month while also having as few debts as possible.

5. Go through as many criminal check databases as possible.

Although the options you read about for confirming data on a tenant can help, they might still hide some details regarding someone's criminal history or background. You must review as many criminal check databases as you can so you can identify problems that a tenant might pose.

Go to federal, state, and county criminal records. Look through sex offender registries as well. All these databases can help you get specific information on what someone might have done in the past. Anyone who does not show up on these databases should be relatively safe.

6. Check with a few of the prior landlords a prospective tenant might have had.

Contact at least two prior landlords that a tenant had. For businesses, ask the manager of any building that the person used to occupy. Ask a few questions about a prospective tenant including:

- Whether or not that person paid the rent on time.

- Why that person moved out; ask if this was an involuntary move or if they were forced to move.

- Whether that person gave a proper advance notice before leaving a property; a renter should give at least 30 days' notice of vacating a property.

- Any damages in one's unit beyond just regular wear and tear.

- How clean a person might have been.

- Any complaints against the person while occupying the property.

Always Follow the FFHA

Follow the rules established by the Federal Fair Housing Act when offering your property for rent. The FFHA states that you cannot discriminate against people who are finding housing options.

The FFHA prohibits people from denying services to possible renters or tenants based on their race or color, their nationality, their religion, or their sexual orientations. You cannot decline renting properties to people based on the familial statuses or disabilities that they might have.

The key of the FFHA is to ensure that all people have a full right to rent a property. People should not be subjected to any restrictions regarding renting a property.

Be sure to follow the FFHA, but also be aware of any additional fair housing rules that might be set up in your local area. The FFHA is a national guideline that all people must follow, but there is a potential that additional rules might be established in the area of your property.

Be Cautious With Tenants

The problem with some tenants is that they might not be trustworthy. They might be rough or hard on your property. Some tenants could engage in illegal activities on your property or be difficult with other tenants.

You have to know what you are doing when considering tenants that might be risky. There are a few things you can do when trying to find tenants that will not be a problem to you:

- Consider how badly a person wants to rent your property.

A person who really wants to rent immediately could make him suspicious. This could be a sign that the person wants to use a property for some questionable and potentially dangerous purpose.

- Be wary of anyone who refuses to allow you to check their background or credit history.

Anyone who refuses to go through a background check or credit history report should be rejected. Such a person might be trying to hide something from you.

- People who might be overly friendly.

Some dangerous tenants might coax their way into your property. They might be very friendly, but they might also be lying to you about their references or their history.

- Parts of a person's application might not be completed.

There is always the chance that an applicant might not fill the application completely. This could be a sign that he/she is trying to hide information about their history. That applicant could be covering up how they were fired from a job or that they do not have a good reference.

- Sometimes a tenant might want to pay the move-in costs in installments.

A person who asks to pay move-in costs in installments might not be able to pay the regular rent. A tenant should be able to pay the first month's rent and a damage deposit before moving into the property. If they cannot, they may not be a good risk to have as a tenant.

- Compare the size of the party moving into a property with the size of that actual property itself.

Some tenants might try to move into a property that is too small for their needs. A family of four might try to rent a property intended for just two people, for example. That family might think it is saving money by doing so. The living conditions might be poor and cramped. There is also the risk of the property suffering damage because of the excess traffic and wear. Tenants that move into overly small properties might be bothersome to other tenants because they might make more noise than necessary.

Establish a Good Policy For the Use of Your Property

Every property that someone rents out needs to have rules. Think about when you were at a hotel in the past. Were there rules stating that you could not do certain things to a room? Maybe it might have listed information on how you would be liable for any damages caused by you.

Even with those rules, you were still allowed to do what you wanted within that room. You just had to ensure those activities were within a few simple boundaries. You can create the same rules for your property.

You must create a policy for what tenants can and cannot do when renting your property. This policy should include rules over noise restrictions, where vehicles can be parked, where visitors must park, and any business-related functions a person can and cannot engage in while in your property. You need to establish as many rules as possible so you have some control over what happens in your property.

The most important thing in your policy should detail limits on the renovations and modifications that a person can make to the property. This is vital if you have a condo, office building, or any other property. You need to keep every unit consistent without any individual area being changed.

Tell renters what they are prohibited from doing like adding new appliances instead of the ones that are already in a property or maybe even painting the walls. Provide as many specifics about what people can and cannot do so they know what is appropriate and what is not permitted.

When a tenant vacates, you want it in the same condition before they rented it.

You do not have to control over the lives of people on your property. However, having limitations ensures that your property will stay protected and that you will not lose money. The rules you establish will not infringe upon anyone's life but still protect your property.

Process All Move-Outs Carefully

There will be times when a person has to vacate a property they are renting from you. When this happens, you must process the move-out accordingly and carefully. You need to inspect everything inside a unit to see that it has not been damaged. You would then return the renter's security deposit if applicable.

You must inspect the floors, walls, counters, windows, doors, closet doors, and appliances. Check the furniture if it was included in the rent. Test all light fixtures, plumbing, and other utilities to see that everything is working.

You should arrange for the inspection with the renter a few days before a person moves out of a property. This is to determine if the renter who is leaving may still be held liable for any repairs you might have to complete in your property.

Friendly Ideas For a Landlord to Consider

You will be operating your rental property as a business, but that does not mean that you will act unkindly or ruthless. Your tenants will appreciate you if you understand their needs and try to reach out to them on occasion. There are a few great ideas that you can use to reach out to your tenants and show that you appreciate them:

- Write a welcome letter to any new tenant.

- Help a tenant learn about the new area that person is moving into. Offer a printout that lists information on local services and attractions.

- Stock the bathrooms in the property initially. This shows that you are thoughtful about their needs.

- Keep an open line of communication whether it is through an office or through email or social media. Use this to answer any questions a tenant might have relating to his unit or the entire property.

- Always have a calm and positive tone when speaking with the tenants. You can encourage them to be themselves so long as they follow the rules listed in any agreements that were made in the past.

Chapter 43: Hiring a Property Management Team

There is a potential that you might not have access to your real estate property. After all, you can invest in anything from any part of the world. You might not be able to clean and maintain the property. This is where the services of a property management team can come in handy.

A property management team is a group responsible for maintaining your property and keeping it ready for use. A team can be hired to clean and restock a rental home, apartment, office or other area in between renters or tenants. A team could also be hired to maintain the outside of a property.

A management team can arrange for new renters and conduct interviews and background checks.

The Management Team

The people who will work as your management team are vital to how well it operates. You should hire people who understand what it takes to keep a property cleaned and appropriately maintained. There are a few important people who can work for such a team:

- A lawn care specialist can be included to help with mowing a lawn, managing the landscape in an area.

- A cleaning staff can thoroughly clean the property. The same staff can also restock the room with additional materials for a tenant's use as needed.

- Outdoor maintenance professionals can work on the painting of the outside of the property, clean the walkways, and even work on windows.

- Technicians for maintaining the heating or air conditioning systems, the electrical system, the water supply, and the plumbing.

- You can hire someone to take care of a pool if your property has one.

- A professional management company can:

    o Interview prospective tenants and do background checks.

    o Receive the rental monies.

    o Arrange for check-outs and refund damage deposits.

    o Make sure the unit is in good condition for the next tenant.

    o Arrange for specialists in plumbing, electricity, painting, etc.

    o Forward rental monies to you.

    o Make arrangements for paying the utility bills.

Your property management team can be versatile and could do almost anything you need done if you are not available to do it yourself. Make sure the team is properly staffed and that the company has an excellent reputation.

When Would a Management Team Attend Your Property?

You would have to establish regular communication with your property management team to ensure that someone attends your property on a regular basis. You might have to schedule the team to get there once or twice a week.

A great rule of thumb is to have the property reviewed before a new tenant arrives. Don't forget to have that team come over a day or two after that tenant leaves so the property can be cleaned properly.

Can the Tenant Do Any Management?

A property management team ensures that the tenant in your property will only be responsible for the day-to-day cleaning of their unit. The renter should still be subjected to rules involving damages and the proper use of the unit. The tenant should be liable for any damages.

A long-term tenant that will stay in a place for months or years will be responsible for cleaning their unit on a regular basis. The management team will help with the outside area and making sure all the utilities work. That team would clean out the individual unit after the tenant moves out and before someone comes in for the first time.

Hiring a Management Team

You can find many property management teams that could help you with fixing up your property and keeping it presentable. There are a few things to consider when you hire a management team:

1. Check the reputation.

2. Screen the entire management staff before hiring.

3. Contact other owners that the maintenance team has worked with in the past.

4. Ask for references..

5. Have the maintenance team complete the National Center for Housing Management's Maintenance Technical Aptitude Test. This test focuses on how well

people can maintain and repair mechanical issues in a property. The test also covers safety points and cleaning steps.

What Will the Service Cost?

You should expect to pay around 10 to 30 percent of the monthly rent cost for your property on a property management firm's expenses. For instance, you might get $5,000 in rent every month from people who use your property. You would then have to spend close to $1,000 each month on your management team. You can always set up your own custom plan for how the maintenance team can be paid, but it is your call as to how a team will be paid.

Having a valuable property management team on hand is vital to your real estate investment. You need to produce a good plan where your property is maintained appropriately so people will be comfortable with your space.

Chapter 44: Heirs to Your Investments

The last point to discuss in this guide involves how your heirs can work with a property you are invested in. One of the best parts of real estate investing is that you can hold onto a property for as long as you want. You could pass your investments to your heirs. This is a great opportunity that ensures your properties will stay in your family after your passing.

The great news about this is that you will give your heirs a unique investment that could be profitable to them in the future. There are a few important things to look into when letting the next generation of your family take control of your investments.

This chapter is important because many people who invest in real estate are seniors who have more money to work with. They might be interested in various properties for retirement use or just to make some extra retirement income. Maybe this could be just for diversifying one's investment portfolio. Regardless, it is not uncommon for people to inherit real estate investments. Anyone who does inherit a property will have many options to consider. However, the taxes associated with it could be a real problem.

A Few Basic Choices

Your heirs will have a few choices for what they can do with any properties they inherit:

1. An heir has the right to sell the property. This might be subjected to various taxes including a capital gains tax.

Your heirs will not have to pay tax on the appreciation that occurred on the property during your lifetime. They will have to pay other taxes based on any gains that were made after the inheritance. In other words, the capital gains tax is based on appreciation after the inheritance, not before.

2. A person could also move into an investment property provided there are no tenants living there.

The taxes associated with the property might be higher due to the higher value of the building. The tax rate that your heirs would pay would be based on the value of the property at the time of the inheritance.

3. Heirs can also rent out those properties. An inherited property can also be used as a vacation rental.

Any depreciation expenses associated with the property can reduce the total taxable income one might have to pay when using the property. However, the depreciation would have to be repaid if the property is sold.

Rules for Taxes

Although your heirs might receive some tax benefits from your investment property, there are a few taxes that will have to be paid regardless. There are four types of taxes that your heirs will have to pay.

Note: This section relates to taxes in the United States. Taxes will vary by country.

Estate Taxes

The estate tax refers to the cost to enact a transfer of a person's estate to an heir. This occurs after the person who owns a property dies and leaves the property to someone in the family or even ant other person.

The good news is that federal estate taxes in the United States are not applied to most estates. An estate would have to be at least $5 million in value to be subjected to the federal estate tax.

Your individual state might have rules for how much state tax you would pay. The estate tax in Illinois can be at least 0.8% while that total is closer to 10% in Washington State. Check the rules in your state to see what estate taxes you might have to pay and if there is a potential for you to avoid them based on the value of the inheritance in question.

Capital Gains Taxes

The capital gains tax is calculated on the profits associated with the property. However, capital gains are taxed based on the value of the property when it was inherited.

When an heir sells a property, that person will pay money based on the gains that occurred after the sale. An agent's commission, if applicable, can be removed from the sale amount in this case. This allows the heir to perhaps report a tax loss.

The heir can hold onto the property for as long as they want. When the value of the property continues to rise, the total amount of capital gains tax that would have to be paid will increase. Anyone who inherits a property will have to calculate the tax applicable after the sale. This is to see if a property is worth holding or if the property should be sold as quickly as possible. Talking with a tax professional for assistance is always in your best interest.

Property Taxes

An heir will have to pay the same property taxes as what the original owner of the investment paid. When the property is transferred to an heir, the investment is assessed at the